T0291326

Culture and Resilience at Work

In 1979, Suzanne C. Kobasa propounded her theory of 'hardiness' in which she hypothesised her 3Cs—commitment, control, and challenge—as the basic ingredients of hardiness that make an individual stress-resilient. She was one of the early researchers who paid attention to personality features and illustrated that individuals who experience high levels of stress without mental and physical illness have a different personality than do those who become ill in stressful conditions. In current times, the discourse has enjoyed a sustained scholarly interest, but there is hardly any study on corporate professionals or the Indian context.

Since the early 1990s, India has joined the corporate world and has been a fast-developing country. This change in the state of affairs provides a broader scope of study on hardy personality in coping with stress in the Indian context. This book examines the efficacy of hardiness on the Indian corporate professionals in the post-globalisation scenario. It endeavours to situate Kobasa's foundational theorisation along with those offered by other scholars in the context of contemporary life situations with a focus on India. It presents a hypothesis that in the Indian context, culture could be looked at as yet another basic component of hardiness.

Culture and Resilience at Work offers an assessment of the significant contribution of Indian culture as one of the major contributing components in enhancing hardiness in corporate professionals. It will be of interest to researchers, academics, professionals, and students in the fields of stress management, human resource management, social psychology, cultural studies, and organisational behaviour.

Pallabi Mund is Assistant Professor in Management at DAV School of Business Management, Utkal University, India.

Routledge Focus on Business and Management

The fields of business and management have grown exponentially as areas of research and education. This growth presents challenges for readers trying to keep up with the latest important insights. *Routledge Focus on Business and Management* presents small books on big topics and how they intersect with the world of business research.

Individually, each title in the series provides coverage of a key academic topic, whilst collectively, the series forms a comprehensive collection across the business disciplines.

Crony Capitalism in US Health Care
Anatomy of a Dysfunctional System
Naresh Khatri

Entrepreneurship Education
Scholarly Progress and Future Challenges
Gustav Hägg and Agnieszka Kurczewska

Optimal Spending on Cybersecurity Measures
Risk Management
Tara Kissoon

Culture and Resilience at Work
A Study of Stress and Hardiness among Indian
Corporate Professionals
Pallabi Mund

For more information about this series, please visit: www.routledge.com/Routledge-Focus-on-Business-and-Management/book-series/FBM

Culture and Resilience at Work

A Study of Stress and Hardiness
Among Indian Corporate Professionals

Pallabi Mund

Routledge
Taylor & Francis Group

NEW YORK AND LONDON

First published 2022
by Routledge
605 Third Avenue, New York, NY 10158

and by Routledge
2 Park Square, Milton Park, Abingdon, Oxon, OX14 4RN

Routledge is an imprint of the Taylor & Francis Group, an informa business

© 2022 Pallabi Mund

Library of Congress Cataloging-in-Publication Data
Names: Mund, Pallabi, 1983– author.
Title: Culture and resilience at work: a study of stress and hardiness
    among Indian corporate professionals/Dr. Pallabi Mund.
Description: New York, NY: Routledge, 2022. | Series: Routledge focus
    on business and management | Includes bibliographical references and
    index.
Identifiers: LCCN 2021014610 (print) | LCCN 2021014611 (ebook) |
    ISBN 9781032023458 (hardback) | ISBN 9781032023465 (paperback) |
    ISBN 9781003182986 (ebook)
Subjects: LCSH: Executives—Job stress—India. | Corporate
    culture—India.| Resilience (Personality trait—India. | Industrial
    psychiatry—India.
Classification: LCC HF5548.85 .M86 2022 (print) | LCC HF5548.85
    (ebook) | DDC 158.7/20954—dc23
LC record available at https://lccn.loc.gov/2021014610
LC ebook record available at https://lccn.loc.gov/2021014611

ISBN: 978-1-032-02345-8 (hbk)
ISBN: 978-1-032-02346-5 (pbk)
ISBN: 978-1-003-18298-6 (ebk)

Typeset in Times New Roman
by Apex CoVantage, LLC

Dedicated to my parents, Dr Subhendu Mund
and Ms Pranati Mund

Contents

Tables

Figures

Abbreviations

CT   Collectivism
DRS   Dispositional Resilience Scale
FC   Family culture
FG   Faith in God
GAS   General Adaptation Syndrome
GRS   General role stress
IRD   Inter-role distance
LOM   Level of management
KY   Karma yoga
PE   Perpetual experience
PIn   Personal inadequacy
RB   Role boundedness
SK   Self-knowledge
SR   Social responsibility
SRD   Self-role distance

Preface

Culture and Resilience at Work: A Study of Stress and Hardiness Among Indian Corporate Professionals is the result of my personal anxiety over the stress which I developed even when I was a postgraduate student of clinical and counselling psychology. As a part of my course curriculum, I counselled persons with psychological disorders and could identify stress as a major cause of most mental health issues. After obtaining my master's in business administration, when I started working with the Human Resources Department of a multinational corporation, I could see how the members of my team and the information technology professionals were struggling to cope with job-related stress, especially role stress, on a daily basis. I wanted to know more about stress and its various aspects. I would wonder why some individuals cope with stress better than others. When I began my academic career and started researching the subject for a PhD, I came across Kobasa's theory of hardiness and her 3Cs. From what I know of Indian family, society, and culture, I hypothesised culture as another 'C' and sought to explore its viability through quantitative research. I am glad that my hypotheses were confirmed: Culture does play a role in creating resilience in individuals, and therefore, it can be another addition to the 3Cs of Kobasa.

I wish to thank all the respondents of this study without whose honest cooperation I could not have completed this study. I have been very lucky to have had a very kind and extremely knowledgeable supervisor in Professor B. B. Mishra, whose constant guidance and support helped me grow through my research work.

My parents, Dr Subhendu Mund and Ms Pranati Mund, have been my real source of inspiration, and it was because of them that I could garner the confidence for writing this book. My father always believed in me more than I do, and it is his confidence in me that has always motivated me. His timely and expert advice and constant support have made all this possible. My son, Advik, who does not exactly know what this is all about, is excited in his own way, and lots of love to him for bearing with the work his mom had been doing.

I am immensely grateful to Brianna Ascher, Naomi Round Cahalin and Christopher Mathews for their ungrudging support and valuable guidance, and it has been a great learning experience working with them.

I am very grateful to Routledge and Taylor & Francis for accepting my work for publication. This is my first book, and needless to say, their acceptance has proved very inspiring to a young scholar like me.

—Pallabi

1 Introduction

This monograph is the outcome of my research on the efficacy of Suzanne C. Kobasa's 3Cs of hardiness (1979a), added with my hypothesis of 'culture' as the fifth C, particularly in the context of Indian corporate professionals. According to Aaron Antonovsky, Kobasa formulated her hypotheses "out of Maddi's existential theory of personality" (1987, p. 35). In turn, Maddi has also acknowledged the role of existential psychology in hardy personality and revealed that he has been depending on this aspect in his clinical practice ('The Story of Hardiness', 2002).

This introductory chapter of this monograph begins with an overview of the main concepts of this study: mainly stress and hardiness and the relationship between them. The theoretical bases of stress and hardiness are also discussed briefly. It also presents a detailed account of the relevance and purpose of the study and the research issues associated with the project. The objectives drawn from the research issues and their respective hypotheses are also included. This chapter also discusses the research methodology, with inputs on the research problem, the type of research, the population considered for this study, the sampling methods undertaken for the study, and how the variables were measured, as well as how the data were collected for the research. A section also deals with the process of investigation and the analytical tools used.

The journey of the studies in hardiness began with explorations into the phenomenon called 'stress'. It has become one of the most widely used terms in today's world, but stress has never been unknown to human beings. We can imagine that human beings must have experienced both physical and mental stress since the time they had to hunt for their food or find shelter for the night. There have been myriad stressors which humankind has had to cope with, but today's competitive world has led stress to unprecedented dimensions.

Stress has been a matter of concern for scientists and researchers of various disciplines: physics, endocrinology, psychology, sociology, physiology, and the like for a long time, especially after industrialisation. *Stress* was used in its lexical sense as early as the 14th century to mean hardship, straits, adversity, or affliction. Experimental physiologist William Bradford Cannon (1871–1945) coined the term "fight-or-flight response" (also called 'hyperarousal' or 'the acute stress response') in his work, *Bodily Changes in Pain, Hunger, Fear, and Rage* (1915, p. 211). He explored the physiology of emotion in *The Wisdom of the Body* (1932) and looked at stress as a disturbance of homeostasis under conditions of cold, lack of oxygen, and so on. *In Bodily Changes in Pain, Hunger, Fear, and Rage*, he focused on traumatic shock, which had been a major issue for soldiers.

Although a section of scholars believe that stress studies and the use of the term have an older history, researches in this area of study became more focused after Hans Selye indicated the concept of stress in his path-breaking seminal work 'A Syndrome Produced by Diverse Nocuous Agents', sent to and published as a 'Letter' in *Nature* (4 July 1936). At the beginning of his career, while experimenting with the strains experienced by living organisms in their struggles to adapt to and cope with changing environments, he had vaguely identified stress. He detected that patients having different ailments often exhibited identical signs and symptoms.

Hans Hugo Bruno Selye (1907–1982), a Hungarian Canadian endocrinologist, turned out to be the pioneering authority in the study of stress for his sustained scholastic contribution to this area of study. Selye also introduced the notion of "eustress" in 1974, which refers to a type of stress that is both physiologically and psychologically positive. Everyone needs a little bit of stress in their life in order to continue being happy, motivated, challenged, and productive. According to Selye, it is when this *stress* is no longer tolerable and/or manageable that *distress* comes in.

Selye also identified the General Adaptation Syndrome (GAS), a response of the body to demands placed on it. This syndrome reveals how stress induces hormonal autonomic responses, and over time, these hormonal changes might lead to ulcers, hypertension, arteriosclerosis, arthritis, kidney disease, allergic reactions, and the like.

Initially, researchers were more concerned over dysfunctional stress which has negative outcomes on an individual's well-being. In the preceding few decades, there has been a growing interest in identifying the variables which reduce the negative impact of life stressors on an individual. It was interesting to find the presence of personality factors which act as mediators or buffers in the stress–illness relationship (Pearlin and Schooler, 1978; Kobasa, 1979a; Wheaton, 1983; McCrae and Costa, 1986).

A significant turning point came in stress studies in 1967 when psychiatrists Holmes and Richard H. Rahe published 'The Social Readjustment Rating Scale' in the *Journal of Psychosomatic Research*. The Social

Readjustment Rating Scale, or SRRS, popularly also known as the Holmes–Rahe Scale listed 43 stressful life events that might contribute to an individual's illness.

This fact is corroborated by Bruce P. Dohrenwend in his paper called 'Inventorying Stressful Life Events as Risk Factors for Psychopathology: Toward Resolution of the Problem of Intracategory Variability' (2006):

> Since the publication of this economical measurement procedure, the SRE, a tremendous increase has occurred in the construction of such measures and in quantitative research on relations between inventoried life events and health. For example, a search of the terms *life events*, *life change*, *stressful life events,* and *life stress* (or a combination of these terms) using PsycINFO (www.apa.org/psycinfo) shows an increasing rate of publications on these topics, from 292 in the decade of 1967 to 1976, to 2,126 in 1977 to 1986, to 4,269 in 1987 to 1996, to 3,341 in the truncated 1997 to 2005 portion of the present decade. This voluminous literature documents that life events are related to a wide variety of physical and psychological problems in both cross-sectional and longitudinal research (e.g., Breslau, 2002; Brown and Hariis, 1978; Dohrenwend and Dohrenwend, 1974; Grant et al., 2004; Gunderson and Rahe, 1974; Paykel, 1974; Rahe and Arthur, 1978).
>
> (p. 477)

The complicity between stressful life events and illness/stress confirmed by SRRS gave a paradigmatic shift to this area of study. Dohrenwend (b. 1927) and his co-researcher, social psychologist and epidemiologist Barbara Dohrenwend (1927–1982), organised the historic conference on 'Stressful Life Events: Their Nature and Effects' at the City University of New York in 1973. The proceedings of the conference came out as a book in 1974.

However, a number of subsequent studies on the relationship between stressful life events and physical illness also observed that many individuals do not fall ill even after undergoing stressful life events, as indicated by the small, although significant, correlations found with larger samples (Rabkin and Struening, 1976). This led to a shift in perceptions that it is less the stress, per se, than the mediational variables which predict physical and psychological outcomes. Thereafter, a major interest developed for mediational variables like coping style (Lazarus and Folkman, 1984) and daily hassles (Kanner et al., 1981) in buffering the adverse effects of stress. Coping refers to strategies directed toward either managing an event appraised as a threat (problem-focused coping) or managing the emotions connected with the threat (emotion-focused coping). Contemporary studies have found significant correlations between various measures of psychological and physical symptoms and style of coping (Pearlin and Schooler, 1978; Billings and Moos, 1981).

A pioneering study by Cobb (1976) provides evidence that supportive interactions among people are protective against the health consequences of life stress. Thus, he defines social support as information leading the subject to believe that one is cared for and loved, esteemed, and a member of a network of mutual obligations. Social support has been considered a significant factor in buffering the effects of stress in animal studies (Bell et al., 1982) and studies focusing on individuals' physical disease (Lynch, 1977), physical health (Nuckolls et al., 1972; Gore, 1978), and psychological distress and disorders (Brown et al., 1975).

In 1979a, there came a significant conceptual turn in stress studies when Suzanne C. Kobasa, propounded the theory of hardiness in her paper, 'Stressful Life Events, Personality, and Health: Inquiry Into Hardiness' (*Journal of Personality and Social Psychology*, 1979a). She gave her '3Cs'—commitment, control, and challenge—as the basic ingredients of hardiness which make an individual stress-resilient.

Kobasa, a doctoral scholar of Salvatore R. Maddi, University of Chicago, developed her hypotheses as a consequence of the studies of her predecessors like Maddi, Bartone, and Antonovsky. Her key paper, 'Stressful Life Events, Personality, and Health: An Inquiry Into Hardiness', a part of her thesis, reveals how her hypotheses had been shaped by the contribution of her preceding scholars like Hans Selye (1956), Averill (1973), Rahe (1974), Holmes and Masuda (1974), Holmes and Rahe (1967), the Social Readjustment Rating Scale (Rahe et al., 1971), and the like. She acknowledges that

> [t]he hardy personality type formulated here builds upon the theorizing of existential psychologists (Kobasa and Maddi, 1977; Maddi, 1975) on the strenuousness of authentic living, White (1959) on competence, Allport (1955) on propriate striving, and Fromm (1947) on the productive orientation.

> (1979a, p. 3)

Since the late 1970s, Kobasa's concepts have been employed and investigated by a number of scholars and researchers, but the relevance of the theory of hardiness has become all the more significant in the contemporary scenario. My research project endeavours to situate Kobasa's theorisation and those offered by other scholars in the context of contemporary life with a focus on India and works on a hypothesis that in the Indian context, culture could be looked on as yet another basic component of hardiness.

1.1 Conceptual Overview

Stress refers to a feeling of physical or emotional tension and a feeling of being unable to cope with anxiety, discomfort, and the demands of a particular situation. It can be a reaction to a short-lived situation, such as being stuck in the traffic while going to catch a flight, or it can also be a longer experience if dealing with relationship problems, the death of a spouse, or some other serious life situation.

Hans Selye had defined stress as "the nonspecific response of the body to any demand made on it" (1976, p. 137). It is Selye (1956), again, who formulated the physiological model of stress reaction and identified individual differences in stress reaction. Later on, as stress was looked on as an unpleasant threat, he had to coin the term "stressors" to distinguish between "stimulus" and "response" (Rosch, 1998, p. 3).

Stress in the workplace has come up as a major concern for the professionals employed in multinational companies in the present-day world. They are challenged by day-to-day stress as they have to achieve predetermined targets and obviously, their work calls for greater efficiency and better performance every month or every week or every day, as the case may be. Working under such stressful condition for a long time can affect the physiological or psychological functioning of an individual. Needless to say, if it is not managed properly, it can be very hazardous to a person's mental and physical well-being.

A considerable amount of research has been done over these years on this increasingly alarming condition, and it is indicative of the fact that stressful life events contribute to physical illness. Citing Holmes and Masuda (1974), Kobasa, in her first study of hardiness, argues that stressful life events evoke "adaptive efforts by the human organism that are faulty in kind or duration, lower 'bodily resistance' and enhance the probability of disease occurrence" (1979a, p. 3).

Although there has been an established link between stress and health, it is also true that individuals respond differently to stress, and many remain healthy even under high-stress conditions. This identification of differential effects of stress on individuals is drawn from Selye's (1956) physiological theory of individual differences in stress reaction. Thereafter, the research attention was diverted to the identification of the moderating or mediating factor which keeps certain individuals healthy even under stressful conditions.

The present work highlights Kobasa's concept of hardiness with special reference to its basic components which constitute making an individual stress-resilient. As mentioned earlier, the concept of hardiness was first proposed as a personality style or pattern associated with continued good health and performance under stress. She was one of the first researchers who paid attention to personality features and showed that individuals who experience a high level of stress without mental or physical illness have a different personality from those who become ill in stressful conditions.

Kobasa's study finds that 'hardy' people are buffered against stressful life situations because they engage in certain affective, cognitive, and behavioural responses. In turn, buffering stressors lead to better overall health. Kobasa characterised hardiness as comprising three components, or the 3Cs, wherein an individual is said to have a sense of commitment (involvement) to oneself and work, a sense of personal control (internal locus of control) over one's experiences and outcomes, and the perception that change represents a challenge and thus should be treated as an opportunity for growth rather than as a threat. Non-hardy persons, in contrast, display alienation (i.e. a lack of commitment), an external locus of control, and a tendency to view change as undesirable.

The concept of hardiness was further developed and tested by Kobasa in collaboration with other pioneering researchers like Maddi (1984). Many interesting findings were also added by Paul T. Bartone (1984, 1989, 1991, 1995), a major researcher in this field of study. Apart from these pioneering researchers, hardiness has also been studied and examined by a number of investigators who have provided useful input to enhance individuals' effectiveness in confronting stress.

A lot of time has passed after Kobasa and her succeeding scholars gave their theories on hardiness. The world of the 1970s overwhelmingly changed after globalisation and the explosion of the information technology. The corporate world has not been the same in the recent years. During the 1990s, India also entered the corporatised and globalised world as a major player. More important, highly skilled Indian youth have entered the scene as software personnel and professionals of various kinds, working for multinational companies all over the world.

In the last decade or so, the situation has become all the more alarming owing to the global economic recession resulting in increased work pressure among professionals to meet deadlines and targets fixed by their employers. In addition to this, people often have to live with different societal roles and are therefore more prone to stress. It is more evident in the Indian context as there has always been pressure on working men and women to justify the multiple roles they have to play, sometimes against their own wishes and abilities. The recent outbreak of COVID-19 has further added to the distressful situation across the globe.

Considering these conditions, it may be hypothesised that hardiness could possibly be the answer to stress resiliency. This study deals with the relationship between role stress and hardiness and the efficacy of hardiness among Indian corporate professionals in reducing the negative effects of stress.

1.2 Theoretical Bases of Role Stress

1.2.1 Sources of Role Stress

Role is based on the role theory developed by anthropologist Ralph Linton in his iconic work *The Study of Man* (1936). He employs a theatrical metaphor to interpret 'role' as the dynamic aspect of status or 'position'. To differentiate between role and status (or position), he says,

> A role represents the dynamic aspect of a status. The individual is socially assigned to a status who occupies it in relation to other statuses. When he puts the rights and duties which constitute the status into effect, he is performing a role.
>
> (p. 114)

As an organisation has its own structure and goals, an individual has their personality and needs. These two interact with each other and get integrated into a role. Thus, role is an integrating point of an organisation and the individual. According to Pareek, each role has its own system, consisting of the role occupant and those who have a direct relationship with the person and, thereby, certain expectations from the role. These significant others having expectations are role senders. They send expectations to the role. As the role occupants also have expectations from their roles, they, too, are role senders. The role occupant and the role senders constantly interact, and the processes of role sending and role receiving together influence the role behaviour of the individual. A person's role behaviour also influences the expectations of the role senders. Thus, a role episode has a feedback loop (Pareek, 1993).

Role stress refers to the stress experienced by a person due to the conflicts arising out of meeting the needs and expectations of the various role senders and which is perceived as difficult to meet. The performance of the role normally satisfies the various needs of the occupants. However, sometimes, it becomes a potential source of stress, too, for the role occupant.

A variety of stressors which exist in the environment the individual lives in lead to role stress. People may face role stress on the job or off the job—mainly at home, other institutions, and communities they are related to. Due to advanced technology, globalization, and industrialisation, the 21st century is often described as the age of stress as there has been a drastic change in the nature of society and the workplace. Due to these radical changes, even the home environment has largely been affected, with an increase in marital and familial discord. Consequently, the nuclear families and issues related to familial ties lead to uncertain fears and insecurities in individuals' lives. These non-work demands in association with work demands can be highly stressful for any individual.

The work demands can be generally divided into task, role, interpersonal, and physical demands. Task demands consist of stresses such as a change in work responsibilities or heavy workload, coping with technological changes, and time pressures like meeting targets or deadlines. Role demands occur when inconsistent or confusing expectations are presented to the employee. Sometimes, interpersonal demands, like harassment, poor leadership, or inappropriateness, and weak relationships with peers, supervisors, and subordinates can arise in a work environment and induce stress in the professionals. At other times, physical demands like harsh, extreme, strenuous, or hazardous work environments can also lead to workplace stress. Even poorly designed jobs and high levels of competition can induce a lot of stressful situations.

Cooper and Marshall (1976) have specified mainly seven sources of organisational stress: factors intrinsic to a job, role in an organisation, career development, organisational interface, organisational structure, the relationship with the organisation, and stressors due to individual differences (personality traits, coping capability, behavioural patterns). Similarly, Burke (1993) has classified job stressors into six categories: physical environment, role stressors, organisational structure and job characteristics, relationships with others, career development, and work–family conflict.

These multiple on-the-job and off-the-job stressors have become the major sources of role stress for an individual. Apart from these factors, there might be some intrinsic factors, such as fear and uncertainty about the future, an individual's attitudes and perceptions about the world, unrealistic expectations, or any major life change, that can also be stressful for an individual. Prolonged stress that arises out of these internal and external factors can lead to severe physical and psychological problems in individuals. Thus, it is quite evident that the three potential factors that can cause role stress are the environment one lives in, the organisation one works for, and the individual themselves.

1.2.2 Role Space Conflicts

This section summarises Pareek's (1993) theory of role stress which has been employed in my study.

Any conflict between the self, the role under question, and other roles occupied by a person are considered as role space conflicts or stress. Various forms of these conflicts include the following:

> **Self-Role Distance (SRD):** When the role a person occupies goes against their self-concept, they experience this kind of stress. This is

essentially a conflict arising out of a mismatch between the person and their job. For instance, an introverted person may have trouble fulfilling the role of a salesperson.

Intra-Role Conflict: Since an individual learns to develop expectations as a result of their socialising and identification with significant others, it is quite likely that they see a certain incompatibility between the different expectations or functions of their roles.

Role Stagnation: With the advancement of the individual, the role changes, and with this change in role, the need for taking up a new role becomes crucial. This problem of role growth becomes acute, especially when an individual occupying a role for a long time enters another role in which they may feel less secure. The new role demands that an individual outgrows the previous one, taking charge of the new role effectively. The stress emerging from this situation is called 'role stagnation'.

Inter-Role Distance (IRD): When an individual occupies more than one role, conflict between different roles is considered IRD. In other words, it is experienced when there is a conflict between organisational and non-organisational roles. More than one role for any role occupant would lead to role conflicts.

1.2.3 Role Set Conflicts

The conflicts arising as a result of incompatibility among the expectations by 'significant' others (and by the individual themselves) are referred to as role set conflicts. Various forms of this conflict include the following:

Role Ambiguity: when an individual does not possess clear cut knowledge about the responsibilities at work.

Role Expectation Conflict: when different role senders impose conflicting demands on a role occupant and the role occupant feels that there are too many expectations from the role senders.

Role Erosion: when a role occupant feels that the functions which they would like to perform are being performed by some other role.

Resource Inadequacy: when the resources either human or materialistic required by the role occupant for performing the role effectively are not available.

Personal Inadequacy (PIn): when the role occupant feels that they do not have the necessary skills and training for effectively performing the functions expected from their role. This is bound to happen when the organisations do not impart periodic training to enable the professionals to cope with the fast changes both within and outside the organisation. This usually happens when these persons are assigned new roles without enough preparation or orientation.

Role Isolation: In a role set, the role occupant may feel that certain roles are psychologically closer to them, while others are at a much greater distance. The main criterion of distance is the frequency and ease of interaction. The stress emerging from the distance referred is called role isolation. The gap between the desired and the existing linkages indicates the amount of role isolation.

Later on, Pareek (2002) added a new role stress—'**role boundedness**' (RB)—as a role space conflict in combination with SRD, IRD, and PIn to develop an index of an individual's role stress which he called the General Role Stress (GRS) scale. According to him, when an individual feels highly obligated to the expectations of the significant role senders and sacrifices their own interests, preferences, values, comforts, and so on, they may be said to be role-bounded. Such a person may experience a conflict between their tendency to live as a person and as a role occupant.

The current study focuses more on exploring the relationship of GRS with other variables used in this study, mainly hardiness and culture.

1.3 Theoretical Roots of Hardiness

Hardiness is looked at as the specifics of what existentialists call existential courage (Maddi, 2004). The existential philosophers and existential psychologists view the world in a constant state of flux, requiring continuous readjustment, particularly concerning stress. In this context, individuals identified as hardy are believed to have a greater capacity for dealing effectively with life's challenges that pertain to responsibility, isolation, and death. Maddi elaborates in 'The story of Hardiness':

> According to existential psychology (Kierkegaard, 1954; May, 1958; Frankl, 1960; Maddi, 1970), meaning of life is not given but rather is created through the decisions people make and implement. Virtually everything we do or fail to do constitutes a decision—big or small; whether we recognize this or not. Needless to say, some decisions are big and others are small. As specific decisions accumulate, more pervasive meaning systems and directions emerge. Once established, meaning systems and directions can be changed only by sharpened awareness and a concerted effort. Whatever their specific content, decisions by their nature require that we choose the future, that is, the path that is relatively unfamiliar, or the past, that is, the path that is relatively familiar.
>
> (2002, p. 175)

According to existential psychology, consistently choosing the future leads to continued personal development and fulfilment and is therefore the most desirable stance. In Maddi's words,

> [w]hat is needed for us to be provoked regularly toward the developmentally more valuable choices for the future is existential courage. For the theologian, Kierkegaard (1954), this courage was the faith that in choosing the future one was drawing oneself closer to God, who is, after all, the prototypical future-chooser. Although also a theologian, Tillich (1952) more recently defined existential courage secularly as self-confidence and life acceptance.
>
> ('Twenty Years of Hardiness Research and Practice',
> 1999, p. 7)

Bartone, another major scholar of hardiness, views hardiness as a broad, generalised perspective (derived from existential psychology) that affects how one views oneself, others, work, and even the physical world:

> The concept of hardiness is not new. It is theoretically grounded in the work of existential philosophers and psychologists such as Heidegger (1986), Frankl (1960), and Binswanger (1963), and involves the creation of meaning in life, even life that is sometimes painful or absurd, and having the courage to live life fully despite its inherent pain and futility. It is a global perspective that affects how one views the self, others, work, and even the physical world (in existential terms, *Umwelt*, the "around" or physical world; *Mitwelt*, the "with" or social world; and *Eigenwelt*, the world of the self or me).
>
> ('Resilience Under Military Operational Stress',
> 2006, p. S137)

In her 'Stressful Life Events, Personality, and Health: Inquiry Into Hardiness' (1979a), Kobasa had affirmed that

> [t]he hardy personality type formulated here builds upon the theorizing of existential psychologists (Kobasa and Maddi, 1977; Maddi, 1975) on the strenuousness of authentic living, White (1959) on competence, Allport (1955) on propriate striving, and Fromm (1947) on the productive orientation.
>
> (p. 3)

She, along with such distinguished co-researchers as Maddi and Kahn, has been consistent in her theory that the characteristic of hardiness is based on the existential theory of personality and is defined as a person's basic stance towards their place in the world that simultaneously expresses commitment, control, and readiness to respond to challenge. She has been striving to establish that an individual who possesses a hardy personality is marked by their way of perceiving and responding to stressful life events that prevents or minimises the strain that can follow stress and that, in turn, can lead to mental and physical illness. In 'Intrinsic Motivation and Health' (1981), inspired by D. E. Berlyne's (1924–1976) concept (1960), Maddi and Kobasa describe "intrinsic motivation" as "an important determinant to survival as well" (p. 299). They also identify intrinsic motivation and existential courage as by-products of hardiness, strengthening the support for existential psychology's underpinnings of this construct.

Kobasa, Maddi, and Kahn further refined the definition of the construct of hardiness as a "constellation of personality characteristics that function as a resistance resource in the encounter with stressful life events. The personality dispositions of hardiness are commitment, control, and challenge" (1982, p. 169). Building on this accumulation of research, Kobasa (1982a) stresses the inclusion of active participation between events, the environment and individuals, and the three interrelated variables taken from existential theory that form its basic foundation—commitment, control, and challenge (the 3Cs of hardiness).

Kobasa further explains that the first C—commitment—is a tendency to involve oneself in, rather than experience alienation from, whatever one is doing or encounters in life. Committed persons have a generalised sense of purpose that allows them to identify with and find meaningful the persons, events, and things of their environment. The second C, or control, is the tendency to think, feel, and act as if one is influential, rather than helpless, in the face of the varied contingencies of life. Persons in control do not naively expect to determine all events and outcomes but, rather, perceive themselves as being able to make a difference in the world through their exercise of imagination, knowledge, skills, and choice. The third C of hardiness is challenge, which is the tendency to believe that change rather than stability is normal in life and that changes are interesting incentives to growth rather than threats to security. Persons with challenge are individuals with an openness to new experiences and a tolerance of ambiguity that enables them to be flexible in the face of change.

In Maddi's perception, in order that existential courage is truly expressed, a person must possess all 3Cs: commitment, control, and challenge. The hardy attitudes structure how you think about your interaction with the world around you and provide motivation to do difficult things. Thus, Maddi views that the combined hardy attitudes of 3Cs constitute the best available operationalisation of existential courage. In Maddi's (2013) words,

> conceptually, all three Cs of hardy attitudes need to be strong, in order to provide the existential courage and motivation to do the hard work

of turning stresses to advantage; that hard work involves hardy coping, hardy social interaction, and hardy self-care (Khoshaba and Maddi, 2004; Maddi, 2002).

(p. 9)

Maddi further explains:

The combination of hardy attitudes, hardy coping, and hardy social interactions facilitates turning stressful circumstances to developmental advantage. In this, one has the courage and strategies that permit (1) clear evaluation of the stressful circumstances, (2) a consequently emerging sense of what can be done to learn from them and increase in capability thereby, and (3) persistence in carrying out what has been learned. This process will reduce the stressful circumstances, and in that way, decrease strain, and the likelihood of breakdowns.

(2013, p. 15)

Thus, the aim of the attitudes and strategies involving hardiness is to recognise stress, learn from it, and thereby move one's living toward wisdom and fulfilment. And this is an ongoing process, not one that, once achieved, indicates that nothing further is required (Maddi, 2013).

1.3.1 Hardiness: Trait or Type

Hardiness is often referred to as a personality variable, but it is largely distinct from the 'Big Five' personality dimensions of openness, conscientiousness, extraversion, agreeableness, and neuroticism (Costa and McCrae, 1992; Digman, 1990). Hardiness was found to be a unique predictor of military cadet performance beyond the variance accounted for by the Big Five factors in a study in which it was examined with the Big Five dimensions (Bartone et al., 2009).

Hence, hardiness, as a personality construct is not fully trait-like or state-like. It is apparently trait-like because it shows a relatively stable quality of individuals and state-like because it can increase or decrease depending on socio-environmental factors and training (Bartone and Hystad, 2010). Likewise, Maddi (1996) also believes that hardiness can be increased or decreased by life experiences. He further explains that in all fully elaborated personality theories, there are some components that are present at birth and others that develop through the interaction of the person with others and situations. There are many conceptualised personality dispositions (e.g., need for achievement, ego-strength, optimism, hardiness) that fit into this later developed category.

1.3.2 The 3Cs of Hardiness

Kobasa (1979a) had stated that the formulation of hardy personality type builds on the theorising of existentialist psychologists (Kobasa and Maddi, 1977) on the strenuousness of authentic living, White (1959) on competence, Allport (1955) on appropriate striving, and Fromm (1947) on the productive orientation.

Commitment

Kobasa posits,

> Staying healthy under stress is critically dependent upon a strong sense of commitment to self. An ability to recognize one's distinctive values, goals, and priorities and an appreciation of one's capacity to have purpose and to make decisions support the internal balance and structure that White and other theorists (cf. Coelho et al., 1974) deem essential for the accurate assessment of the threat posed by a particular life situation and for the competent handling of it.
>
> (1979a, p. 4)

Bartone rightly observes that Kobasa's understanding of commitment is based on certain features of Antonovsky's (1974, 1979) "sense of coherence" which also entails commitment and involvement with others and lends resistance to the negative impact of stress which Kobasa has also acknowledged (1979a, p. 3). In a recent paper, Bartone, along with his co-authors, has reiterated his conviction that commitment is "the abiding conviction that life is interesting and worth living" (2017, p. 499).

Similarly, Maddi, a lifelong champion of hardiness, reaffirms in *Hardiness: Turning Stressful Circumstances Into Resilient Growth* (2013) that commitment is "the belief that no matter how bad things get, it is important to stay involved with whatever is happening, rather than sink into detachment and alienation" (p. 8).

Control

According to Kobasa, "[h]ardy persons are considered to possess . . . the belief that they can control or influence the events of their experience" (1979a, p. 3). The control facet of hardiness propounded by Kobasa follows the study of Averill (1973), which demonstrated that some organisms are not hampered by stressful stimuli and that the highly stressed person is healthy due to certain characteristics like decisional control, cognitive control, and coping skills. In other words, when subjects are given control over aversive stimuli, the stress effects are substantially reduced compared to when the aversive stimuli are uncontrollable.

Kobasa acknowledges that her idea of control has been formed after her preceding scholars: (Lefcourt, 1973; Rodin and Langer, 1977; Rotter et al., 1962; Seligman, 1975). Her idea of control, therefore, shows similarities to Rotter's concept of locus of control (Rotter et al., 1962) and Lefcourt's (1973) control beliefs.

Kobasa and the other scholars have identified control as something which comes from within and a hardy individual wins over stress even in adverse conditions by striving to successfully cope with adversity. Maddi (2016) asserts, "Control is the belief that even in difficult circumstances, it is best to keep trying to have an effect on outcomes, rather than slipping into powerlessness".

Challenge

The third C of hardiness is, in Kobasa's words, "the anticipation of change as an exciting challenge to further development" (1979a, p. 1). Kobasa's impression of challenge has been primarily influenced by Fiske and Maddi's (1961) work on the importance of variety in experience, and Maddi's (1967) ideas on engagement versus alienation. In 'The Existential Neurosis' (1967), Maddi used the term "ideal identity" (p. 318) to describe the person who lives a vigorous and proactive life, with an abiding sense of meaning and purpose, a belief in their own ability to influence things, and an appreciation for variety and change in experience. This is contrasted with the "existential neurotic" (p. 313), who shies away from change, seeking security and predictability in the environment.

The influence of existential theorists is evident here as well, as the person high in hardiness is more courageous in choosing to look forward and take action in a world that is inherently unpredictable. Thus, the challenge factor of hardiness involves an appreciation for variety and change in the environment and a motivation to learn and grow by trying new things.

Maddi succinctly defines challenge as "the belief that life is by its nature stressful, and that working on these stresses leads you to learn and grow in the process" (2016).

Maddi and Harvey sum up the concept of hardiness as follows:

> It is the interactive combination of commitment, control and challenge that defines hardiness as the existential courage to face stressful circumstances openly and directly, and the motivation to do the hard work of dealing with them constructively (e.g. Khoshaba and Maddi, 2001; Maddi, 2002). Important in this constructive process is hardy,

of transformational coping (Maddi and Kobasa, 1984), which involves interpreting each stressful circumstance that is encountered as a problem that needs to be solved by your ingenuity.

(2005, p. 410)

In other words, Kobasa's concepts of hardiness and the 3Cs may be looked at as a significant addition to the extant theories and findings in this area of study. Moreover, it has relevance to the present-day world and needs to be re-interpreted and re-examined in terms of the stress-related conditions of the corporate professionals.

1.4 Relevance of the Study

During the 1970s, a considerable corpus of research on adult individuals indicated that stressful life events contribute to physical illness (Dohrenwend and Dohrenwend, 1974; Gentry and Kobasa, 1984; Rabkin and Struening, 1976). To reduce the negative effects of stress on physical and psychological health, understanding the nature of the relationship between stress and illness and the forces that moderate this relationship is crucial. A number of factors have emerged through research that appear to moderate the negative effects of stress on physical and psychological health, such as Cobb's social support (1976), the structure of coping (Pearlin and Schooler, 1978) and the types of coping styles (Lazarus and Folkman, 1984). A few other moderating factors that act as stress-resilient mechanism such as "self-efficacy" (Bandura, 1977) and "sense of coherence" (Antonovsky, 1979, p. 186) were also explored.

Thereafter, much of the health promotion research began to focus on identifying those resistant factors that contribute to long-term health. The focus shifted from psychopathology and weaknesses caused by stress towards strengths that might assist individuals in their daily functioning and promote their well-being. During this time, Kobasa (1979a) introduced the concept of hardiness, projecting it as a personality disposition which acts as a buffering system and reduces the ill outcomes of stress. As a result, the individual remains healthy and strong even in high-stress situations.

In the last few decades, pressure in the workplace has considerably increased and has resulted in more stress-prone illnesses among professionals working in the corporate sector. There is a need to control the detrimental effects of stress on the professionals' physiological and psychological health. Considering these developments, it is important to study the efficacy of hardiness in buffering the negative consequences of stress among Indian corporate professionals.

1.5 Purpose of the Study

In the present competitive and target-oriented world, controlling stress among professionals and having a healthy life is of utmost importance. In order to control stress, we need to explore various factors which can assist an individual to effectively manage its harmful consequences. A number of psychologists, sociologists, scientists, and psychopathologists have come up with typical findings which have grown in magnitude all these years.

While learning about the identification, reactivity, and approach towards stress in relation to personality types, I came across the theory of hardiness, a personality disposition which acts as a moderator between stress and its negative outcomes that can cause serious damage to one's physiological and psychological well-being. Surprisingly, however, a large portion of studies on hardiness and its effects on various subjects of different age groups are mostly done in the United States and other developed countries, neglecting India to a major extent. Reasons may vary as to why it has not been considered as an important concept of study till today insofar as India is concerned. In such a situation, it would be interesting to study how hardiness helps today's stressed-out Indian professionals working in the corporate sector in coping with stress. This will, in turn, help professionals identify a particular role stressor (or stressors) and manage it through hardiness. Consequently, it will help in maintaining long-term good health, improved productivity, and job satisfaction among the professionals.

1.6 Major Research Issues

1.6.1 Limited Study on Hardiness in India

As already indicated, it is noteworthy to mention that a large body of research on hardiness has been done in the context and work situation of the United States and few other developed countries but very limited research in India. Since the early 1990s, India has joined the corporate world and has been a fast-developing country. Moreover, the women of our country have also come forward and have been quite visible in the corporate world both in quality and quantity. This changed state of affairs provides a broader scope of study on hardy personality in coping with stress in the Indian context.

1.6.2 Overlooking the Importance of the Study of Hardiness on Indian Corporate Professionals

Apparently, Indian professionals working in different corporate sectors have been suffering from a lot of stress, resulting from either intrinsic or extrinsic factors. A good number of studies have been directed towards the hardy coping style of military personnel, police, health professionals, academicians, students, adolescents, older adults, teachers, and the like, but very few studies have dealt with the problems faced by today's stressed-out corporate professionals. Besides, there has hardly been any such study pertaining to the Indian context. Therefore, the foremost purpose of this study would be learning the positive effects of hardiness in reducing stress in Indian corporate professionals.

1.6.3 Limiting the Importance of the Effect of Gender on Hardiness

It may be pointed out here that except for a few studies, since its inception, hardiness has been mostly studied on male subjects, neglecting women's mediating effects on stress–illness–hardiness relationships. Moreover, there has hardly been any study of Indian female professionals working in the corporate sector. Often results obtained from studies in men have been generalised as outcomes for women. This has raised a questionable concern on the differential effects of gender on hardiness. This issue needs to be addressed and an attempt should be made to study the variance in hardiness across gender.

1.6.4 Limited Progress in Revaluating the Possibility of an Additional Trait (or Traits) to the Basic Ingredients of Hardiness

In addition to Kobasa's three Cs—challenge, commitment, and control—Salvatore R. Maddi and others have added connection, social support, courage, and conditioning, among others, as the fourth C of hardiness. It appears that Maddi has added 'connection' as the fourth C of the hardy traits. Unfortunately, try as I might, I could not locate the primary source where he discussed this. Nancy Stek mentions that "[c]onnection . . . surfaced in Maddi's work" as "a fourth 'C'" (2014). Similarly, Natalie L. Hill, a professional therapist, also mentions 'connection' as the fourth C, by which she means "social support" (2013). However, she does not mention Maddi. On the web site of KGA, a human resources services firm, "connection" has been mentioned as "a fourth attitude".

Mark Gorkin, a licensed clinical social worker and author, in his undated blog introduces "conditioning" as the fourth trait in what he calls the "Four C's of Psychological Hardiness". By conditioning, he implies "regular aerobic exercise or physical conditioning" (www. mentalhelp.net/blogs/building-stress-resilience-and-organizational-hardiness-despite-doing-quot-more-with-less-quot/).

However, in recent scholarship, the importance of connection, that is social support, has been identified as a trait in individuals for bouncing back and resisting stress (Thompson, 2007). Even in her early papers, Kobasa had indicated the significance of connection. In 'Personality and Resistance to Illness' (1979b), a paper based on her doctoral dissertation, Kobasa enumerates social support as one of the "additional factors" (p. 421). Similarly, in 'Who Stays Healthy Under Stress?' (Kobasa et al., 1979), another paper based on her dissertation, the efficacy of "social support" (p. 595) is highlighted.

As a certified clinical psychologist, Maddi, a major hardiness scholar and founder of the Hardiness Institute, recognises the importance of therapy and explains how and why people get well in therapy strongly relates to the connection between the client and therapist. In a community, the power of belonging and connectedness provided by its members leads to greater success in mutual aid and self-help groups. Maddi and his co-researchers have been reiterating the need for interpersonal relationships which come from social support—giving and receiving assistance and encouragement to each other and between employees or friends or members of a family (Maddi et al., 2002; Maddi and Khoshaba, 2001a, 2005).

The world has not been what it was four decades back when Kobasa propounded her concept of hardiness. Consequent to globalisation, liberalisation, the information technology (IT) revolution, and unprecedented growth of the corporate sector, as well as the cosmopolitisation of human life and living, the way we look at work, family, society, and life in general has undergone a sea-change. Therefore, it is now necessary to re-evaluate the extant principles and seek new dimensions of strategies for coping with stress under the umbrella of hardiness. In view of the changed and changing scenario of workplaces all over the world, we need to explore the possibility of the presence of another trait (or traits) which could as well be looked on as a component (or components) of hardiness.

Hypothetically, a strong background and upbringing of **culture** can be a contributing factor to the formation of a hardy personality. However, the role of culture in the shaping of an individual's personality, hardy or otherwise, has not been adequately or convincingly studied so far. As India has a very ancient and unique culture, which is enriched by its essential multiculturalism, I have hypothesised the possibility of **culture as the fifth component**, a contributing factor for a hardy coping style in addition to the 3Cs of Kobasa and the (unconfirmed) fourth C of Maddi.

1.7 Objectives

The objectives of my research work are as follows:

Objective 1: To find out the relationship between hardiness and its components with various role stresses of Indian corporate professionals

Objective 2: To assess the impact of various socio-demographic factors on the hardiness of corporate professionals

Objective 3: To assess the impact of various socio-demographic factors on the four role stresses experienced by Indian corporate professionals

Objective 4: To assess the relationship between hardiness and its 3Cs with various aspects of Indian culture

Objective 5: To assess the difference, if any, in the level of role stress, hardiness, and cultural aspects with respect to the two sectors—IT and banking—and two cities—Bengaluru and Bhubaneswar

1.8 Hypotheses of the Study

On the basis of the objectives of this study, the hypotheses drawn are as follows:

Hypothesis 1: There is a meaningful correlation between hardiness and its 3Cs with the various role stresses of the corporate professionals.

Hypothesis 2: There is an impact of the various socio-demographic factors on the hardiness of corporate professionals.

Hypothesis 2a: Women professionals have stronger effects of hardiness than do their male counterparts.

Hypothesis 2b: The elderly professionals have greater hardiness than do young ones.

Hypothesis 3a: Women professionals experience greater role stresses than their male counterparts do.

Hypothesis 3b: Married professionals experience greater role stresses than do unmarried ones.

Hypothesis 3c: Elderly professionals perceive more stressful situations compared to younger professionals.

Hypothesis 4: Certain aspects of Indian culture contribute to making hardy professionals.

Hypothesis 5: There will be a significant difference between the professionals' level of role stress, hardiness, and various cultural aspects with respect to both sectors (IT and banking) and cities (Bengaluru and Bhubaneswar).

1.9 Research Methodology

Any research sets off with a research problem or an issue over a given phenomenon or a set of phenomena. Research is basically undertaken to establish or confirm facts, re-affirm the results of previous work, solve new or existing problems, support certain theories (already established), or develop completely new theories. It is basically a creative investigation which is done systematically, based on already-existing ideas and concepts or developing a new idea or concept for the advancement of one's knowledge.

1.9.1 Research Problem

The present study is about the relationship between stress and hardiness and the efficacy of culture as a hardiness trait in reducing stress among Indian corporate professionals.

1.9.2 Research Design

The research design for this study is descriptive. As the very term implies, descriptive research designs are used when the researcher wants to describe specific behaviour as it occurs in the environment. Sometimes these are also called 'correlational' or 'observational' studies. In this project, I have tried to establish the correlation between stress and the hardiness of Indian professionals working in the corporate sector. As the study involves a one-time interaction with groups of people, it is a cross-sectional descriptive study.

1.9.3 Type of Descriptive Research Method

To achieve the research objectives, this study followed the descriptive correlational (survey) design as the focus was to learn the relationship between variables. The survey method is also referred to as the questionnaire method which involves the collection of primary data about subjects, usually by selecting a representative sample of the population or universe under study, through the use of a questionnaire. It allows for the standardisation and uniformity in both the questions asked and the method used for approaching subjects, making it far easier to compare and contrast answers by the respondent groups. It also ensures higher reliability than some other techniques.

In this study, the respondents were given a predetermined set of questions that are related to the specific domain and the correlated aspects of the research. The respondents for this study were professionals working in the corporate sector who were sent the composite questionnaire by email. The procedure and guidelines for filling out the questionnaire were provided in the information sheet. The professionals had to follow the guidelines, fill out the questionnaire, and 'submit' their responses.

1.9.4 Sample Unit

The sample unit included professionals of two corporate sectors—banking and IT—from two cities: Bengaluru and Bhubaneswar in India. The units of the sample for this study were as follows:

- Banks: Axis Bank, HDFC Bank, ICICI Bank, and Canara Bank
- IT companies: Tech Mahindra, Infosys, Wipro, and TCS

1.9.5 Sampling Method

The sample for this study was drawn through a purposive sampling technique. A purposive sample is a non-probability sample based on the characteristics of a population and the objective of the study. It is also known as judgemental, selective, or subjective sampling technique as the researcher relies on their own judgement when choosing the sample. In purposive sampling, personal judgement needs to be used when choosing cases that help answer research questions or achieve research objectives. According to Black, purposive sampling is a non-probability sampling method, and it "occurs when elements selected for the sample are chosen by the judgment of the researcher. Researchers often believe that they can obtain a representative sample by using a sound judgment, which will result in saving time and money" (2010, p. 215). Besides, this sampling technique proves quite effective when, due to the nature of research design and its objectives, a limited number of people serve as primary data sources.

1.9.6 Sample Size and Sample Distribution

The composite questionnaire was e-mailed to 320 professionals who were purposively selected (160 professionals from each sector—banking and IT), including both men and women. Four companies each for banking and IT were chosen, and the questionnaire was distributed equally across sectors and cities. For example, out of 160 banking professionals, 40 professionals from each bank (4 banks) and 20 (out of 40) from each city were emailed the questionnaire.

Some of the questionnaires were rejected due to missing values in the instruments used, and a few questionnaires did not come back as they were not attempted by the respondents. This resulted in a final sample size of 234 professionals (120 from the banking sector and 114 from the IT sector). The city-wise distribution had 123 professionals belonging to Bengaluru (64 banking and 59 IT) and 111 (56 banking and 55 IT) belonging to Bhubaneswar.

The composite questionnaire also had a section seeking details about the various socio-demographic factors, such as gender, age, marital status, tenure in the current job, and level of management (LOM), included in this study. Based on gender, the total sample consists of 51% males and about 49% females. Nearly 44% of the sample consists of professionals younger than 30, about 46% professionals between 30 and 40 years, and the remaining 10% were older than 40. Married professionals (68%) are more represented than unmarried ones (32%). Middle-level professionals (59%) constitute the highest percentage of the sample, compared to those at the junior level (24%) and the senior level (17%) of management. Based on tenure, about 23% are professionals who have served a tenure of less than 1 year, 43% have served a tenure between 1 and 5 years, 18% have a tenure between 6 and 10 years, and 16% have a tenure of more than 10 years.

The following pie charts show the pictorial representation of the sample distribution based on various socio-demographic factors for both sectors and cities of this study.

Figure 1.1 depicts the sample distribution of the various socio-demographic factors for both sectors and cities.

1.9.7 Sources of Data

The data for the present study were obtained from both primary and secondary sources.

Primary Data

The primary data are the data collected for the first time, keeping in view the objective of the investigation. The primary data for this study were collected through the psychometric instruments and data sheet for socio-demographic factors from the professionals of two corporate sectors—banking and IT—covering two cities, Bengaluru and Bhubaneswar, in India. The socio-demographic data sheet was used to record the socio-demographic and personal details of the respondents. All the professionals were emailed a structured questionnaire which included items about GRS, hardiness, and culture to retrieve data related to the objectives. The questionnaires served as the most helpful tool for the data collection of my research.

Secondary Data

The secondary data for this research was collected from various databases like EBSCO, JSTOR, ProQuest, Inflibnet, and Google Website, and other published books and journals.

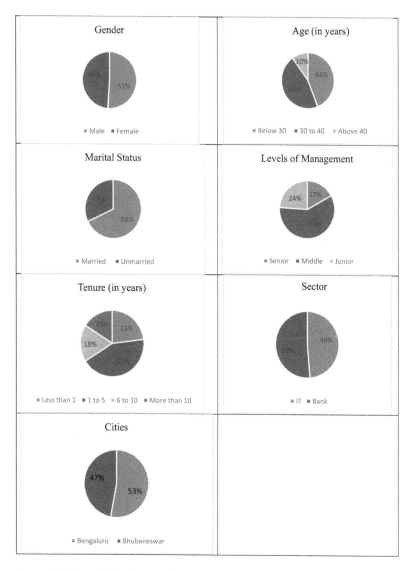

Figure 1.1 Sample Distribution of Various Socio-Demographic Factors

1.9.8 Measurement Tools Used

Based on the objectives, there were mainly three scales of measurement used in this study. The types of measurement scales, their components/parameters, and their scoring are explained in the following subsections.

Stress

To measure stress, this study used the standardised scale of GRS developed and tested by Udai Pareek (2002). This scale gives a general index of an individual's role stress, focusing on their role space stresses. The main stresses in this category are SRD, IRD, RB, and PIn. It is self-administered, and the respondent rates 12 items on a 5-point scale varying from 1, *Never or scarcely feel this way*, to 5, *Frequently or always feel this way*. The scoring was slightly modified to have uniformity in scale and have Likert scale measurements for all tools.

Scoring of the GRS

The scoring for the GRS scale was also modified a little in accordance with the need of this study. GRS is measured on a Likert scale, ranging from 1 to 5, which contains three items each of the four role space stresses. Questions 1, 5, and 9 are related to SRD; 2, 6, and 10 are related to IRD; 3, 7, and 11 are related to RB; and 4, 8, and 12 are related to PIn. Scoring for a particular role stress would range from 3 to 15, and the overall score would range from 12 to 60. The weighted average of the respondents' ratings for each role stress was obtained for analysis.

Hardiness

To measure hardiness, a modified scale of 18 items has been used in the present study that gives a general index of hardiness and scores for each component of hardiness. These 18 items include 6 items from each component of hardiness—commitment, control, and challenge—rated on a 5-point Likert scale varying from 1, *Not at all true*, to 5, *Completely true*. This hardiness scale is an adapted version of Bartone's (1995) Dispositional Resilience Scale–15 (DRS-15), which has been modified to suit our study and relate it to the Indian context. It gives a measure of the individuals' overall hardiness as well as the scoring of the three main components of hardiness (commitment, control, and challenge).

Scoring of the Hardiness Scale

The hardiness instrument used in this study is an 18-item scale based on a 5-point Likert scale, ranging from 1, *Not at all true*, to 5, *Completely true*, which contains six items each of the three main components of hardiness. Questions 1, 4, 7, 10, 13, and 16 are related to commitment; 2, 5, 8, 11, 14, and 17 are related to control; and 3, 6, 9, 12, 15, and 18 are related to challenge. The total score for a particular component would range from 6 to 30, and the overall hardiness score would range from 18 to 90. The weighted average of the respondents' ratings for each component, as well as the overall hardiness score, was also obtained for analysis.

Culture

A new scale of 14 items was constructed to measure the cultural aspect of corporate-sector professionals. The scale was developed keeping in view the various aspects of Indian culture. The scale has two items each related to seven different aspects of our Indian culture like collectivism (CT), karma yoga (KY), family culture (FC), faith in God (FG), perpetual experience (PE), self-knowledge (SK), and social responsibility (SR).

The meaning of each dimension is explained in the following.

CT is the moral stance, political philosophy, ideology, or social outlook that emphasises the group and its interests. It is the opposite of individualism. Collectivists focus on communal, societal, or national interests in various types of political, economic, and educational systems. According to Harry C. Triandis (2001), CT has two aspects: "horizontal collectivism" and "vertical collectivism". In horizontal CT, equality is emphasised and people engage in sharing and cooperation, whereas in vertical CT, hierarchy is emphasised and people submit to specific authorities.

It is important to point out here that CT is one of the four dimensions of Hofstede's cultural dimensions theory (2001). In a CT culture, individuals identify themselves with a group. They believe that the desire and goals of their group are more important than anyone else's individual ideas. Thus, they are more connected to their group and care less about personal goals as individuals and more about combined goals as a whole group. In a collectivist society, people value their in-group as a whole, taking into account how their actions give a positive or negative impression to outgroups while staying tightly knit with their in-group (2001, p. 225).

According to Hofstede (1983), individualism–CT is the major construct between Eastern and Western societies. CT is "a set of feelings, beliefs, behavioural intentions, and behaviours related to solidarity, concern for others, cooperation among members of in-group and the desire to develop a feeling of groupness with other members (Hui, 1988; Lebra, 1976)" (Kapoor et al., 2003, p. 687). In general, Asian cultures, such as Chinese, measure high on CT as they emphasise cooperation, interdependence, and harmony. They are more concerned with the consequences of their behaviour on their in-group members and are more likely to sacrifice personal interest for the attainment of collective interests (Hofstede, 1983; Chan and Goto, 2003). In contrast, "[i]ndividualism refers to the tendency to view one's self as independent of others and to be more concerned about consequences of behaviors of one's personal goals" (Thomas et al., 2003, p. 455).

KY

The concept of KY, the guiding principle of Indian life, has been given by Sri Krishna, looked on as an incarnation of Vishnu, the Supreme Lord, in the *Bhagavadgita*, which forms a part of the Mahabharata by Vyasa:

Karmaṇyevādhikārastemāphaleṣhukadāchana
mā karma-phala-heturbhūrmātesaṅgo'stvakarmaṇi
(2:47)

In S. Radhakrishnan's rendering, "[t]o action alone hast thou a right and never at all to its fruits, let not the fruits of action be thy motive; neither let there be in thee any attachment to inaction" (p. 119). This teaches that we have to perform our duty, but we are not entitled to the fruits of our action. *Niskama KY, or KY,* teaches us to perform our actions without expecting any fruit or reward. According to Radhakrishnan (1888–1975), a renowned philosopher and interpreter of Indian metaphysics and the scriptures, who is also a former president of India, "[d]oing one's duty without expecting any result or taking pride over the success makes one attached to Karma. Hence, there is no anxiety or remorse". In his historic Upton Lectures (Oxford University, 1926), Dr Radhakrishnan explains: "The theory of Karma recognises the rule of law not only in outward nature, but also in the world of mind and morals" (The Hindu View of Life, p. 72). The individual is only the means to an end: The person is doing their work in accordance with the laws of nature or the wish of God—this forms the basic ideology with which an Indian worker supposedly acts ("*Nimittamatram bhava Sabyasachin*": *Bhagavad Gita* 11:33).

Thus, for an Indian, "[k]arma is not a mechanical principle but a spiritual necessity. It is the embodiment of the mind and will of God. God is its supervisor, *karmadhyakshah*" (1927, p. 72).

FC

Indian societal culture believes in family and social life. Even now one can see, in both rural and urban areas, two to three generations of a family living under the same roof. In India, the tradition of living in a joint family and being a part of even the extended family plays a significant role in the formation of the culture of sharing and caring. Although the changing patterns of contemporary life require living apart, there is always an emotional bonding and togetherness among the people. As Nandan and Eames (1980) have rightly pointed out,

[f]amilies in India are tied up with unseen bond, cooperation, harmony and interdependence. Togetherness is what rules over here. There has

been a long-standing tradition in the Indian culture to live in extended families. The joint family has always been the preferred family type in the Indian culture, and most Indians at some point in their lives have participated in joint family living.

(p. 20)

FG

In Indian culture, God is not an entity far away from the mundane world or the individual's life. God is a living presence which guides an individual in every step of life. According to Dr Radhakrishnan, "[r]eligion is not the acceptance of academic abstractions or the celebration of ceremonies; but a kind of life or experience" (1947, p. 15).

Referring to the Census Report of India for 1911, Dr Radhakrishnan (1947) cites the observation of Mr Burns: "The general results of my inquiries is that the great majority of Hindus have a firm belief in one supreme God, Bhagavan, Paramesvara, Isvara, or Narayana". Dr Radhakrishnan further cites Sir Herbert Risley (1851–1911) from his *The People of India* to demonstrate the familiarity of common Indians on religious ideas and God:

These ideas are not the monopoly of the learned, they are shared in great measure by the man in the street. If you talk to a fairly intelligent Hindu peasant about the Paramatma, Karma, Maya, Mukti, and so forth, you will find as soon as he has got over his surprise at your interest in such matter, that the terms are familiar to him, and that he has formed a rough working theory of their bearing of his own future.

(1927, pp. 55–56)

PE

Indian culture imbibes and encourages *Swadhyaya* (self-study) in an individual for *jnana*: knowledge and wisdom. Although, traditionally, it has been the sacred duty of a Brahmin to engage in the creation, dissemination and perpetuation of knowledge, basic learning and reading habits are encouraged by every class/caste. In the past, as the scriptures or spiritual texts were normally in Sanskrit, the common people representing the other castes were not always able to read them. In course of time, these Sanskrit texts were translated or adapted in the various Indian languages with local and temporal interpretations. There have also been folk traditions by which the common people got to listen to the scriptures through *Purana Pandas* or *kathaks* (interpreters of scriptures) or folk performances like *pandvani, Hari Katha, jatras, leelas, nautanki*, and the like. In Odisha, the tradition of *Bhagabata Ghara/Tungi* can also be taken as an example. In the Indian tradition, when a bride goes to her in-laws' place after her wedding, along with other gifts, she is also given some religious books. In this way, the essence of the spiritual belief percolated beyond texts and reached one and all. The habit of reading or listening to noble thoughts not only improves the wisdom and world view of an individual but also helps them in building their character and personality. That is why Dr Radhakrishnan says, "Reading a book gives us the habit of solitary reflection and true enjoyment" (1927, p. 77).

SK

The tenets of KY and *Atmajnana* (SK) are mutually inclusive. On the basis of the Upanishads, the 9th-century seer and commentator Sankaracharya wrote a treatise called *Atmabodha*. This work on Advaita Vedanta or the philosophy of non-dualistic Vedanta has been translated and presented as *Atmabodha*, or SK, by Swami Nikhilananda (1996). According to him, "Self-Knowledge is vital. All other forms of knowledge are of secondary importance; for one's action, feeling, reasoning, and thinking are dependent upon one's idea of the self. One's view of life will be either materialistic or spiritual according to one's conception of oneself".

SR

The Indian culture and tradition believe in CT of a unique kind. The following words of Radhakrishnan explain the value of SR in Indian culture: "What shall it profit a man if he gain[s] the whole world but lose[s] his own soul? A Sanskrit verse reads: "For the family sacrifice the individual; for the community the family; for the country the community, and for the soul the whole world" (1927, p. 90).

Radhakrishnan clarifies: "So, while Hinduism does not interfere with one's natural way of thinking, which depends on his moral and intellectual gifts, education and environment, it furthers his spiritual growth by lending a sympathetic and helping hand wherever he stands" (1927, p. 49).

Swami Vivekananda (1863–1902) also believed that God is present in everybody's heart. In his preaching and songs, he advised serving the living God present in the human temple. His saying "Service to mankind is service to God" was also famously followed by Mahatma Gandhi, the Father of the Indian Nation.

Thus, Indian culture teaches an individual to sympathise and empathise with other individuals in the society and that they have a responsibility for everyone else in the world.

Scoring of the Culture Scale

This scale consists of 14 items, 2 items for each dimension of culture. It is self-administered, and the respondent rates the 14 items on a 5-point Likert scale varying from 1, *Strongly disagree*, to 5, *Strongly agree*. An overall score for each respondent would vary from 14 to 70. The weighted average score of each respondent for each parameter was measured for the analysis of the study. An average score which is greater than 3 for respondents would mean the professional having a higher cultural value.

1.9.9 Tools and Techniques Used for the Study

The Statistical Package for Social Sciences (SPSS) Version 16.0 has been used to analyse the data in this project. A scale reliability test was first done for all the newly constructed and modified scales to check whether the scale had good reliability and could be considered for further testing on the professionals in this sample. Then descriptive statistics and inferential statistics were applied to the data. While the descriptive statistics described and summarised the sets of data (through means and standard deviations), inferential statistics were helpful in generalising from a sample to a whole population by testing hypotheses.

The frequency distributions, percentage analysis, and a few other techniques, such as correlation, analysis of variation (ANOVA), and post hoc ANOVA, were used in this study. Correlation helped in understanding the relationship between two or more variables in a linear fashion. It also helped in determining the presence, direction, and magnitude of the relationship between the independent and dependent variables of the study.

While correlation helped explain the association or relationship and interrelationships between variables, ANOVA helped with comparing the relationship between two variables across more than two groups. This technique examines the means of subgroups in the sample and analyses the variance between the group means as well. Post hoc ANOVA was used to identify which paired mean differences were responsible for the ANOVA result. When required, the post hoc ANOVA test was also used to identify which group mean (or means) resulted in a significant difference in comparison to the others. This technique precisely helped me confirm the significant effect between the various mean groups.

1.9.10 Preliminary Reliability Analysis of the Newly Constructed Instruments in This Study

To fulfil the objectives of this study, mainly three instruments were used. As mentioned earlier, besides Pareek's GRS scale, which is a standardised scale, the other two instruments related to hardiness and culture were either modified or newly constructed for the present study. To test the reliability of the latter two instruments, this study measured Cronbach's alpha coefficients for each instrument for the 234 participants. Cronbach's alpha is a measure of internal consistency, that is, how closely related a set of items are as a group. It is considered to be a measure of scale reliability. A 'high' value for alpha does not imply that the measure is unidimensional. The alpha coefficient for each scale has been mentioned in **Table 1.1**.

The rule of thumb is that a Cronbach's alpha of .70 and above is good, .80 and above is better, and .90 and above is best. The results show a high internal consistency and an acceptable scale reliability which confirm that these scales are good enough to be used further in the research.

1.9.11 Scope and Limitations

Scope

The present research has been done on corporate professionals working in the banking and IT sectors in Bhubaneswar and Bengaluru. Both the cities were included in my analysis to identify and explain any difference (if at all) that would exist among the corporate professionals in terms of their stress, hardiness, and cultural values.

Limitations

• Sampling was limited to professionals working in the IT and banking sectors in Bengaluru and Bhubaneswar only. Therefore, there would be a limited generalisation of its findings with reference to other occupations.
• The target population was adult professionals; therefore, the sample size was limited to adult corporate professionals only.
• Certain company policies restrict professionals to provide any information about their job-related aspects. Therefore, only a few companies or banks which did not have such restrictions were chosen, especially when the information obtained would be used only for academic purpose.

Table 1.1 Alpha Coefficients for Hardiness and Culture Scales

Instrument/scale	Number of items	Cronbach's alpha coefficients of reliability
Hardiness	18	0.907
Culture	14	0.741

Source: Primary data.

- Basically, some individuals have the habit of not revealing the whole truth while providing their responses, so the ratings obtained may not be true to the core.
- Respondents have a tendency to overrate or underrate a few items in self-report measures which may lead to biased responses and can affect the overall findings of this study.
- The questionnaires were emailed to the respondents, due to which I could get a response rate of only 73% of the total number of questionnaires.

References

Allport, G. W. (1955). *Becoming: Basic considerations for a psychology of personality*. Yale University Press.

Antonovsky, A. (1974). Conceptual and methodological problems in the study of resistance resources and stressful life events. In B. S. Dohrenwend and B. P. Dohrenwend (Eds.), *Stressful life events: Their nature and effects* (pp. 245–255). Wiley.

Antonovsky, A. (1979). *Health, stress and coping*. Jossey-Bass.

Antonovsky, A. (1987). *Unraveling the mystery of health: How people manage stress and stay well*. Jossey-Bass.

Averill, J. R. (1973). Personal control over aversive stimuli and its relationship to stress. *Psychological Bulletin, 80*(4), 286–303. https://doi.org/10.1037/h0034845

Bandura, A. (1977). Self-efficacy: Toward a unifying theory of behavioural change. *Psychological Review, 84*, 191–215.

Bartone, P. T. (1984). Stress and health in Chicago Transit Authority bus drivers. Dissertation, Department of Behavioral Sciences, University of Chicago.

Bartone, P. T. (1991). Development and validation of a short hardiness measure. Paper presented at the Third Annual Convention of the American Psychological Society, Washington, DC. HYPERLINK "http://www.hardiness-resilience.com" www.hardiness-resilience.com

Bartone, P. T. (July 1995). A short hardiness scale. Paper presented at the Annual Convention of the American Psychological Society, New York. www.hardiness resilience.Com

Bartone, P. T. (January 2006). Resilience under military operational stress: Can leaders influence hardiness? *Military Psychology, 18*(Suppl.), S131–S148. DOI: 10.1207/s15327876mp1803s_10

Bartone, P. T., Johnsen, B. H., Eid, J., Laberg, J. C., and Snook, S. A. (2009). Big five personality factors, hardiness, and social judgment as predictors of leader performance. *Leadership and Organizational Development Journal , 30*(6), 498–521. http://dx.doi.org/10.1108/01437730910981908l

Bartone, P. T., and Hystad, S. W. (2010). Increasing mental hardiness for stress resilience in operational settings. In P. T. Bartone, B. H. Johnsen, J. Eid, J. M. Violanti, and J. C. Binnendijk (Eds.), *Enhancing human performance in security operations: International and law enforcement perspectives* (pp. 257–272). Charles C. Thomas.

Bartone, P. T., Johnsen, B. H., Eid, J., Hystad, S. W., and Laberg, J. C. (2017). Hardiness, avoidance coping, and alcohol consumption in war veterans: A moderated-mediation study. *Stress and Health, 33,* 498–507. DOI: 10.1002/smi.2734

Bartone, P. T., Ursano, R. J., Wright, K. M., and Ingraham, L. H. (1989). The impact of a military air disaster on the health of assistance workers: A prospective study. *Journal of Nervous & Mental disease, 177*(6), 317–328.

Bell, R. A., LeRoy, J. B., and Stephenson, J. J. (1982). Evaluating the mediating effects of social support upon life events and depressive symptoms. *Journal of Community Psychology, 10*(4), 325–340. https://doi.org/10.1002/1520-6629(198 210)10:4<325::AID-JCOP2290100405>3.0.CO;2-C

Billings, A. G., and Moos, R. H. (1981). The role of coping responses and social resources in attenuating the stress of life events. *Journal of Behavioral Medicine, 4*(2), 139–157. https://doi.org/10.1007/BF00844267

Black, K. (2010). *Business statistics for contemporary decision making* (10th ed.). West Pub. (1st published 1994, Wiley).

Burke, R. J. (1993). Organizational-level interventions to reduce occupational stressors. *Work & Stress: An International Journal of Work, Health &Organisations, 7*(1), 77–87. DOI: 10.1080/02678379308257051

Cannon, W. B. (1915). *Bodily changes in pain, hunger, fear, and rage.* Appleton-Century-Crofts.

Chan, D. K. S., and Goto, S. G. (2003). Conflict resolution in the culturally diverse workplace: Some data from Hong Kong employees. *Applied Psychology, 52*(3), 441–460. DOI: 10.1111/1464-0597.00143

Cobb, S. (1976). Social support as moderator of life stress. *Psychosomatic Medicine, 38,* 300–314.

Cooper, C. L., and Marshall, J. (1976). Occupational sources of stress: A review of the literature relating to coronary heart disease and mental ill health. *Journal of Occupational Psychology, 49,* 11–28.

Costa, P. T., Jr., and McCrae, R. R. (1992). *The revised NEO Personality Inventory (NEO PIR) and NEO Five Factor Inventory (NEO-FFI) professional manual.* Psychological Assessment Resources, Inc.

Digman, J. M. (February 1990). Personality structure: Emergence of the five-factor model. *Annual Review of Psychology, 41,* 417–440. https://doi.org/10.1146/annurev.ps.41.020190.002221

Dohrenwend, B. P. (2006). Inventorying stressful life events as risk factors for psychopathology: Toward resolution of the problem of intracategory variability. *Psychological Bulletin, 132*(3), 477–495. https://doi.org/10.1037/0033-2909.132.3.477

Dohrenwend, B. S., and Dohrenwend, B. P. (Eds.) (1974). *Stressful life events: Their nature and effects.* Wiley.

Fiske, D. W., and Maddi, S. R. (Eds.) (1961). *Functions of varied experience.* Dorsey Press.

Fromm, E. (1947). *Man for himself: An inquiry into the psychology of ethics.* Rinehart.

Gentry, W. D., and Kobasa, S. C. (1984). Social and psychological resources mediating stress-illness relationships in humans. In W. D. Gentry (Ed.), *Handbook of behavioural medicine* (pp. 87–116). Guilford Press.

Gore, S. (1978). The effect of social support in moderating the health consequences of unemployment. *Journal of Health and Social Behavior, 19*(2), 157–165. DOI: 10.2307/2136531

Hill, N. L. (17 January 2013). The 3 Cs of stress hardiness. *Practice Wisdom.* http://
    practicewisdom.blogspot.com/2013/01/the-3-cs-of-stress-hardiness.html#:~:
    text=There%20is%20a%20fourth%20%22C,do%20you%20see%20stress%
    2Dhardiness%3F
Hofstede, G. (December 1983). Culture's consequences: International differences in
    work-related values. *Administrative Science Quarterly, 28*(4), 625–629.
Hofstede, G. (2001). *Culture's consequences: Comparing values, behaviors, institu-
    tions, and organizations across nations* (2nd ed.). SAGE Publications.
Holmes, T. H., and Masuda, M. (1974). Life change and illness susceptibility. In B. S.
    Dohrenwend and B. P. Dohrenwend (Eds.), *Stressful life events: Their nature and
    effects.* John Wiley & Sons. http://dx.doi.org/10.1037/1061-4087.51.2.95
Holmes, T. H., and Rahe, R. H. (1967). The social readjustment rating scale. *Journal
    of Psychosomatic Research, 11*(2), 213–218. https://doi.org/10.1016/0022-3999
    (67)90010-4
Kanner, A. D., Coyne, J. C., Schaefer, C., and Lazarus, R. S. (1981). Comparison
    of two modes of stress measurement: Daily Hassles and uplifts versus major life
    events. *Journal of Behavioural Medicine, 4*, 1–39.
Kapoor, S., Hughes, P. C., Baldwin, J. R., and Blue, J. (2003). The relationship of
    individualism-collectivism and self-construals to communication styles in India
    and the United States. *International Journal of Intercultural Relations, 27*, 683–
    700. https://doi.org/10.1016/j.ijintrel.2003.08.002
Khoshaba, D. M., and Maddi, S. R. (2004). *HardiTraining: Managing stressful
    change* (5th ed.). Hardiness Institute.
Kobasa, S. C. (January 1979a). Stressful life events, personality, and health: Inquiry
    into hardiness. *Journal of Personality and Social Psychology, 37*(1), 1–11.
Kobasa, S. C. (1979b). Personality and resistance to illness. *American Journal of
    Community Psychology, 7*(4), 413–423. https://doi.org/10.1007/BF00894383
Kobasa, S. C. (1982a). Commitment and coping in stress resistance among law-
    yers. *Journal of Personality and Social Psychology, 42*(4), 707–717. https://doi.
    org/10.1037/0022-3514.42.4.707
Kobasa, S. C., Hilker, R. R. J., and Maddi, S. R. (September 1979). Who stays
    healthy under stress? *Journal of Occupational Medicine, 21*(9), 595–598.
Kobasa, S. C., and Maddi, S. R. (1977). Existential personality theory. In R. Corsini
    (Ed.), *Current personality theory* (pp. 243–76). Peacock.
Kobasa, S. C., Maddi, S. R., and Kahn, S. (1982). Hardiness and health: A prospec-
    tive study. *Journal of Personality and Social Psychology, 42*, 168–177. http://
    dx.doi.org/10.1037/0022–3514.42.1.168
Lazarus, R. S., and Folkman, S. (1984). *Stress, appraisal and coping.* Springer.
Lefcourt, H. M. (1973). The function of the illusions of control and freedom. *Ameri-
    can Psychologist, 28*, 417–425.
Linton, R. (1936). *The study of man.* Appleton-Century-Crofts, Inc.
Lynch, J. J. (1977). *Broken heart: The medical consequences of loneliness.* Basic
    Books, Inc.
Maddi, S. R. (1967). The existential neurosis. *Journal of Abnormal Psychology, 72*,
    311–325. DOI: 10.1037/h0020103
Maddi, S. R. (1975). The strenuousness of the creative life. In I. A. Taylor & J. W.
    Getzels (Eds.), *Perspectives in creativity.* Chicago: Aldine.

Maddi, S. R. (1996). *Personality theories: A comparative analysis* (6th ed.). Waveland Press (1st published 1989).

Maddi, S. R. (20–24 August 1999). Twenty years of hardiness research and practice. Paper presented at the 107th Annual Convention of the APA. https://files.eric.ed.gov/fulltext/ED435061.pdf

Maddi, S. R. (2002). The story of hardiness: Twenty years of theorizing, research and practice. *Consulting Psychology Journal: Practice and Research, 54*(3). 173–185. DOI: 10.1037//1061-4087.54.3.175

Maddi, S. R. (2004). Hardiness: An operationalization of existential courage. *Journal of Humanistic Psychology, 44*(3), 279–298.

Maddi, S. R. (2013). *Hardiness: Turning stressful circumstances into resilient growth.* Springer Briefs in Psychology. DOI: 10.1007/978-94-007-5222-1_2

Maddi, S. R. (August 2016). Hardiness is negatively related to gambling. *Open Access Library Journal, 3*, e2250. http://dx.doi.org/10.4236/oalib.1102250

Maddi, S. R., and Harvey, R. H. (2005). Hardiness considered across cultures. In P. T. P. Wong and L. C. J. Wong (Eds.), *Handbook of multicultural perspectives on stress and coping* (pp. 409–426). Springer. DOI: 10.1007/0-387-26238-5_17

Maddi, S. R., and Khoshaba, D. M. (2001a). *HardiSurvey III-R: Test development and instruction manual.* Hardiness Institute.

Maddi, S. R., and Khoshaba, D. M. (2005). *Resilience at work: How to succeed no matter what life throws at you.* American Management Association.

Maddi, S. R., and Kobasa, S. C. (1981). Intrinsic motivation and health. In H. I. Day (Ed.), *Advances in intrinsic motivation and aesthetics* (pp. 299–321). Springer. https://doi.org/10.1007/978-1-4613-3195-7_12

Maddi, S. R., and Kobasa, S. C. (1984). *The hardy executive: Health under stress.* Dow Jones-Irwin. https://doi.org/10.1016/S0022-3182(86)80108-X

McCrae, R. R., and Costa, P. T. (1986). Personality, coping, and coping effectiveness in an adult sample. *Journal of Personality, 54*, 385–405.

Nandan, Y., and Eames, E. (1980). Typology and analysis of the Asian-Indian family. In P. Saran and E. Eames (Eds.), *The new ethnics: Asian Indians in the United States* (pp. 20–22). Praeger.

Nikhilananda, S. (1996). *Self-knowledge.* Translation with notes of Sankaracharya's *Atmabodha* (pp. 788–820). Ramakrishna-Vivekananda Center of New York. www.ramakrishna.org/catalog/archive/self_knowledge.htm.

Nuckolls, K. B., Cassel, J., and Kaplan, B. H. (1972). Psychosocial assets, life crisis and the prognosis of pregnancy. *American Journal of Epidemiology, 95*, 431–441. https://doi.org/10.1017/ CBO9780511759048.007

Pareek, U. (1993). *Making organizational roles effective.* Tata McGraw-Hill.

Pareek, U. (2002). *Training instruments in HRD and OD* (2nd ed.). Tata McGraw Hill.

Pearlin, L. I., and Schooler, C. (1978). The structure of coping. *Journal of Health and Social Behavior, 19*, 2–21.

Rabkin, J. G., and Struening, E. L. (1976). Life events, stress, and illness. *Science, 194*, 1013–1020. DOI: 10.1126/science.790570

Radhakrishnan, S. (1927). The Hindu view of life. George Allen & Unwin Ltd.

Radhakrishnan, S. (1947). *Religion and society.* London: George Allen & Unwin Ltd.

36 *Introduction*

Rahe, R. H., Lundberg, U., Theorell, T., & Bennett, L. K. (1971). The Social Read-justment Rating Scale: A comparative study of Swedes and Americans. *Journal of Psychosomatic Research, 51,* 241–249.

Rodin, J., & Langer, E. J. (1977). Long-term effects of a control-relevant intervention with the institutionalized aged. *Journal of Personality and Social Psychology, 35,* 897–902.

Rosch, P. J. (1998). Reminiscences of Hans Selye, and the birth of "stress". *Stress Medicine, 14,* 1–6. https://doi.org/10.1002/(SICI)1099-1700(199801)14:1<1::AID-SMI777>3.0.CO;2-W

Rotter, J. B., Seeman, M., and Liverant, S. (1962). Internal versus external control of reinforcement: A major variable in behavior theory. In N. F. Washburne (Ed.), *Decisions, values, and groups* (vol. 2, pp. 473–516). Pergamum Press.

Seligman, M. E. P. (1975). *Helplessness.* San Francisco: Freeman.

Selye, H. (1936). A syndrome produced by diverse nocuous agents. *Nature, 138* (3479), 32.

Selye, H. (1956). *The stress of life.* McGraw-Hill Book Company.

Selye, H., (1974). *Stress Without Distress.* New York: American Library.

Selye, H. (1976). Stress without distress. In G. Serban (Ed.), *Psychopathology of human adaptation* (pp. 137–146). Springer. https://doi.org/10.1007/978-1-4684-2238-2_9

Stek, N. (11 December 2014). Stress-hardiness: The path to resilience for lawyers. www.njlap.org/AboutStress/StressHardinessfullarticle/tabid/83/Default.aspx

Thomas, D. C., Au, K., and Ravlin, E. C. (August 2003). Cultural variation and the psychological contract. *Journal of Organizational Behavior, 24,* 451–471. https://doi.org/10.1002/job.209

Thompson, C. (2007). Improving hardiness in elite rugby players. Thesis submitted for the Degree of Doctor of Applied Psychology (Sport), Victoria University, Australia. http://vuir.vu.edu.au/34210/1/THOMPSON%20Campbell%20-%20 thesis_nosignatures.pdf

Triandis, H. C. (December 2001). Individualism-collectivism and personality. *Journal of Personality, 69*(6), 907–924. https://doi.org/10.1111/1467-6494.696169

Wheaton, B. (1983). Stress, personal coping resources, and psychiatric symptoms: An investigation of interactive models. *Journal of Health and Social Behavior, 24,* 208–229.

White, R. W. (1959). Motivation reconsidered: The concept of competence. *Psychological Review, 66*(5), 297–333. https://doi.org/10.1037/h0040934

2 Literature Review

2.1 Introduction

In Chapter 1, I sought to summarise the discourse on stress with reference to hardiness and the hypotheses related to the project. The concept of hardiness is basically related to that of stress and that it still engages scholars and therapists even 40 years after Suzanne C. Kobasa (née Ouellette) introduced the construct as a personality trait (1979a), indicating its continuing acceptance and efficacy.

Kobasa held that hardiness potentially moderates the impact of stress on physical and psychological health. Her research demonstrated that the high-stress/low-illness group of executives showed a higher level of hardiness in comparison to the high-stress/high-illness group of executives. This theory of Kobasa provides a link to Selye's eustress theory as only those executives showing higher levels of hardiness who had high but positive stress levels, which led to a positive impact on their overall physiological health. Therefore, it can be deduced that hardiness is mostly observed when individuals are under eustress rather than distress.

Hardiness, as a stress-moderating construct, has been addressed both theoretically and empirically by various researchers to date. The main purpose of this chapter is to review the theoretical and empirical attempts to identify the role of hardiness in moderating/ mediating/buffering the impact and ill effects of stress on the physical and psychological health of individuals. Therefore, it is necessary to look at the literature related to stress, followed by the link between stress and illness, and the inception of the moderating effects of personality and hardiness in buffering the ill effects of stress. This chapter also includes discussions about the measurement inequality of the construct of hardiness and the controversial studies based on gender differences and hardiness. Furthermore, the socio-demographic effects on hardiness are also analysed in this chapter.

2.2 Post-1970s Stress Studies

It was Lawrence E. Hinkle, Jr. (1918–2012) who gave a turn to stress studies by using stress in the context of the physical sciences. However, contesting the prevailing concept of stress in the first half of the 20th century, he observed that it was applied to biological and social systems because it appeared to provide an explanation for the apparently 'non-specific' effects of biologic agents and for the occurrence of illness as a part of the response of people to their social environment. Hinkle further averred:

> Evidence subsequently accumulated has confirmed that a large proportion of the manifestations of disease are produced by reaction of the host and not directly by the "causal agents" of disease, and that the components of the host's reactions are not in themselves "specific" to any given "causal agent"; it has confirmed that reactions of people to other people, or to the social environment may influence any physiological process or any disease; but it has also indicated that the concept of "stress" does not provide an adequate explanation for these phenomena.
>
> (1974, p. 335)

Studies on stress were carried forward in a new direction by several other distinguished scholars who looked at the issue from many different angles. Richard S. Lazarus (1922–2002), the author of *Psychological Stress and the Coping Process* (1966) and Susan Folkman (b. 1938), in their iconic work *Stress, Appraisal, and Coping* (1984), studied stress in a systematic and scientific way while introducing the coping and appraisal mechanisms for dealing with stress. These two eminent psychologists held that stress could not be seen as a "stimulus"—something of a pure biological nature rather as a reciprocal influence between an individual and their environment. According to Lazarus and Folkman, psychological stress is "a particular relationship between the person and the environment that is appraised by the person as taxing or exceeding his or her resources and endangering his or her well-being" (1984, p. 19). They further argued that both stress reactions and coping efforts are determined by the way an individual perceives a situation. Thus, they define coping in a certain situational approach "constantly changing cognitive and behavioral efforts to manage specific external and/or internal demands that are appraised as taxing or exceeding the resources of the person" (1984, p. 141). Folkman and Lazarus developed a scale to measure coping, the WCC, or Ways of Coping Checklist.

The later additions to the discourse are primarily explained in terms of the occurrence of events consensually regarded as stressful (Holmes and Masuda, 1974) or defined rationally by reference to both the person and environment (Lazarus and Launier, 1978). While some researchers use stress to denote a stimulus, others use stress to denote a response, and still others view stress as an interactional phenomenon.

2.3 Stress and Illness

The relationship between stress and illness took quite a long time to be established. In scientific studies, the term *stress* was used mostly in physics to describe the force that produces strain on a physical body. It is believed that Selye found it suitable to describe the condition he discovered and borrowed the term. Physicians looked at stress in a slightly different way, hypothesising that stress is a stimulus or event which could potentially lead to adverse effects on health. However, in the last four decades of the 20th century, a large body of literature found that stress plays a precipitating role in the onset of physical and psychological disturbances.

As already indicated, the relationship between the exposures to stressful life events (i.e. circumstances requiring adaptation) and the subsequent onset of illness became the primary focus (Dohrenwend and Dohrenwend, 1984). Rahe (1974) also identified correlations between stressful events and physical illness. Kobasa's 'Stressful life events, personality, and health: An inquiry into hardiness' (1979a) also continued the discourse.

Dr Laura Asbell (1988), a clinical psychologist, defines daily hassles in her dissertation as the minor stressful events and demands that characterise everyday transactions. According to her,

> [a]nother proposed mediating factor in the stress-illness relationship is daily hassles (DeLongis et al., 1982; Kanner et al., 1981; Monroe, 1983). Daily hassles are defined as the minor stressful events and demands that characterize everyday transactions. Studies have shown self-reports of daily hassles to predict concurrent psychological (Kanner et al., 1981) and somatic symptoms (DeLongis et al., 1982), and controlling for initial symptom levels, to predict prospective psychological symptoms (Monroe, 1983). Several mechanisms have been proposed to account for this relationship (DeLongis et al., 1982; Kanner et al., 1981; Lazarus, 1984; Lazarus and Folkman, 1984; Monroe, 1983): hassles could be a measure of external stressors that add up to reach a stress threshold; they might be outcomes of ineffective coping; they could represent an appraisal style such that hassles measures identify people who are more vigilant. However, the mechanism preferred by Lazarus and his group was that hassles were the result of a systemic process that combines all of the above mechanisms. As such, hassles would be a reflection of an interaction involving external

events, appraisal style and quality of coping. However, methods used to study daily hassles have not allowed any conclusive finding over any distinctive mechanism which might be the most befitting in the stress-illness process.

(p. 3)

Quite a few studies were focused on other important stress-moderating variables such as social support and personality (Maddi, 1990). A pioneering study by Cobb (1976) provides evidence that supportive interactions among people are protective against the health consequences of life stress. Thus, he defines social support as information leading the subject to believe that one is cared for and loved, esteemed, and a member of a network of mutual obligations. Social support has been considered a significant factor in buffering the effects of stress in animal studies (Bell et al., 1982). There were also studies focusing on individuals' physical disease (Lynch, 1977), physical health (Nuckolls et al., 1972; Gore, 1978) and psychological distress and disorders (Brown et al., 1975). DeLongis and Holtzman (2005) have foregrounded the importance of both personality and social support in every aspect of stress and coping with stress.

2.4 Stress and Personality

It has been universally accepted now that an individual experiences stress only when the particular situation is assessed as being threatening (De Jong and Emmelkamp, 2000) and that this perception largely depends on one's personality type. This reveals the uniqueness of each individual's personality type, which leads to the changed perceptions in determining stress and, hence, the varying effects in its physical and psychological outcomes. This hypothesis posits that some individuals may have a stress-resistant personality, whereas others may be having a stress-prone personality disposition. The most common stress-prone personality is identified as the 'Type A' personality.

In *Type A Behaviour and Your Heart* (1959), cardiologists Meyer T. Friedman and Ray H. Rosenman reported the results of a longitudinal study of 10 years of 3,000 healthy middle-aged men (ages 35–59). They characterised people with a Type A personality as high-achieving 'workaholics' who multitask, push themselves with deadlines, and hate both delays and ambivalence: therefore, they have a sense of time urgency in order to finish the tasks assigned to them. People with a Type B personality, a perfect contrast to those with Type A, generally live in a lower stress level and are patient, relaxed, easy-going, and, at times, lacking an overriding sense of urgency. Because of these characteristics, Type B individuals are often described as apathetic and disengaged by individuals with Type A or other personality types. Eight-and-a-half years later, Friedman and Rosenman again contacted their sample to examine them for evidence of heart disease. The group labelled Type A on the basis of observable and reported behaviours was found to have twice the rate of coronary heart disease as those whose behavioural patterns were called Type B.

To further establish their own theory of personality, Friedman and Rosenman (1974) did a longitudinal study for 8 years on 3,200 male participants who were asked to answer certain questionnaires. Based on their responses, they evolved a 'Type C personality' classification, in addition to the Type A and Type B personalities. Type C has been described as a personality which involves a passion for work and a desire to achieve goals (typical of Type A), but when faced with stress, the person becomes apathetic (typical of Type B). The participants were then included in the second part of the study 8 years later, to assess how they responded to stress during that period. The results showed that 257 of all the participants had suffered from coronary heart diseases, a group of illnesses wherein stress is the most common cause. It was also concluded that people who are classified in Type B had responded to stress better than those in Type A as 70% of the 257 participants had a Type A personality. The study by Blatny and Adam (2008) provides an outline of the present state of knowledge of the 'C-type' or cancer-prone personality which is primarily based on the fact that specific links between cancer and certain personality traits have not been confirmed. However, there has not been enough study on the Type C personality as compared to the Type A and Type B personalities.

Richard J. Contrada's (1989) study found that Type A individuals were associated with significantly enhanced systolic and diastolic blood pressure (SBP and DBP, respectively) elevations and the Type B showed the least DBP reactivity.

For several decades, it was considered that individuals possess one of the three main personality types: Type A, Type B, and Type C, which is reflected when they approach and react to stressful situations. Generally, Type B is looked on as a stress-resistant personality type, and Types A and C (Helpless–Hopeless) are referred to as stress-prone personalities, causing more psychosomatic, psychological, and physiological problems.

Yet another personality type, Type R, also referred to as 'sensation seekers', was developed by Marvin Zuckerman (1971). Sensation seekers are people who seek thrills and sensations and take calculated risks in their endeavours. To assess this trait, Zuckerman created a personality test called the Sensation Seeking Scale, which assesses the individual differences in terms of sensory stimulation preferences. Zuckerman hypothesised that people who are high sensation seekers require a lot of stimulation to reach their optimal level of arousal. When the stimulation or sensory input is not met, the person finds the experience unpleasant and stressful.

In 2005, while demonstrating the role of psychosocial and behavioural risk factors in the aetiology and pathogenesis of cardiovascular disorders, L. Sher investigated a newly proposed personality construct called the Type D, or the 'distressed', personality. However, there is less substantial theoretical evidence to support the Type D personality theory.

The original research on Type A was based on entirely male samples, but the Type A prototype cannot be considered a personality profile which many women can easily identify with. It does not deny the fact that there are female counterparts who are over-aroused, overstressed, high risk-takers, and high achievers who experience intense time pressure. In *The Type E Women: How to Overcome the Stress of Being Everything to Everybody* (1986), H. B. Braiker interprets the Type E coping style as involving the resentment and frustration produced by continually putting others' needs ahead of one's own: being everything to everybody, which inevitably creates feelings of hostility.

Studies focusing on the relationship of stress with different personality factors also emerged subsequently which indicated personality traits like openness, extraversion, and agreeableness; internal locus of control; mastery; self-esteem; cognitive appraisal (positive interpretation of events and cohesive integration of adversity into self-narrative); and optimism, all evidently contributing to resiliency in stress. When it was established in various studies by pioneering researchers that personality types, or traits, and dispositions have a major impact on how a person confronts and manages stressful situations, "[i]ntegrating various theoretical and empirical leads," Kobasa, Maddi and Kahn report, "Kobasa (1979a) proposed that hardiness is a constellation of personality characteristics that function as a resistance resource in the encounter with stressful life events" (1982, p. 169). Originally projected as a stress-resilient personality disposition, hardiness was developed as a means of explaining why, in the face of stressful events, some individuals become incapacitated while others flourish. According to Kobasa, "[t]his personality difference is best characterized by the term *hardiness*" (1979a, p. 3). Thus, hardiness came up as the term which describes and explains individual differences in stress reactions. The following section explains in detail the relationship between stress and hardiness (personality disposition) and how hardiness helps individuals in being stress-resilient.

2.5   Stress and Hardiness

While a section of researchers were engaged in the study of the psychosomatic and psychological effects of stress on individuals, there were a few who identified stress-resilient personality dispositions which helped individuals in having a healthy coping style. This led to the study of resilient factors which enable a person to stay strong and healthy in adverse situations. It is Kobasa (1979a) and Antonovsky (*Health, Stress and Coping,* 1979) who steered the research away from illness and pathology to "resistance resources". Antonovsky, a professor of medical sociology, coined the term "the salutogenic model" (1979) which demonstrates the relationship between health, stress and coping. Salutogenesis is a medical approach which focuses on the factors that help maintain human health and well-being rather than on factors that cause disease (pathogenesis). While Antonovsky's theory rejected the traditional medical-model dichotomy separating health and illness, it held the relationship as a continuous variable, what he called the "*health ease-dis/ease continuum, or breakdown continuum*" (p. 67).

On the other hand, Suzanne C. Kobasa introduced psychological hardiness as a factor that provides resilience and resistance to stress and its ill effects. In her path-breaking paper titled 'Stressful Life Events, Personality, and Health: An Inquiry Into Hardiness' (1979a), Kobasa characterised hardiness as a personality structure which includes three important components: (a) a commitment (involvement) to oneself and work, (b) a sense of personal control (internal locus of control) over one's experiences and outcomes, and (c) the perception that change represents challenge and thus should be treated as an opportunity for growth rather than as a threat. Non-hardy persons, in contrast, display alienation (i.e. a lack of commitment), an external locus of control, and a tendency to view change as undesirable.

According to Kobasa, individuals high in hardiness are hypothesised to be better able to withstand the negative effects of life stressors and, consequently, are less likely than individuals low in hardiness to become ill. Their resistance to illness presumably results from perceiving life changes as less stressful (Kobasa, 1979a) or from having more resources at their disposal to cope with life changes (Kobasa, 1982a). In support of this hypothesis, Kobasa et al. (1982) found that hardy executives were more likely to remain healthy under conditions of high stress than were non-hardy executives.

In her foundational study, Kobasa (1979a) used a sample of middle- and upper level male executives of a large public utility company. Out of this sample, two groups were identified who had comparably high degrees of stressful life events in the previous 3 years, as measured by the Schedule of Recent Life Events and the Social Readjustment Rating Scale (Holmes and Rahe, 1967). One group ($n = 86$) suffered high stress without falling ill, whereas the members of the other group ($n = 75$) reported becoming sick after their encounter with stressful life events. Illness was measured by the Wyler, Masuda, and Holmes Seriousness of Illness Rating Scale (1970). Hardiness was measured by 15 various scales covering all three components of hardiness. The subjects were asked about three demographic characteristics: age, job level (third, fourth, fifth, and officer), and number of years spent at the current level. Executives were also asked to rate on a scale of 1 (*not at all stressful*) to 7 (*extremely stressful*) how stressful they usually think each of the following areas of life is: work, financial concerns, social/community involvements, interpersonal relationships, family, and personal or inner-life concerns.

A discriminant function analysis, run on half of the participants in each group and cross-validated on the remaining cases, supported the prediction that the high-stress/low-illness participants scored significantly lower on nihilism, external locus of control, powerlessness, alienation from self, and vegetativeness than did high-stress/high-illness participants. These results were enhanced by the fact that various demographic characteristics such as age, education, and socio-economic level failed to discriminate between the two groups. Thus, the results of this study supported the hypothesis that one's personality may have something to do with staying healthy despite considerable stress and defined five instruments that best differentiated the high-stress/high-illness and high-stress/low-illness groups.

Utilising a prospective design of 5 years of study, Kobasa et al. (1981) used a subject pool of middle- and upper level management male personnel of a large public utility to investigate the mediating effects of personality-based hardiness (commitment, control, and challenge) and constitutional predisposition (parents' illness) on the stressful life events–illness relationship. Stressful life events, hardiness, and constitutional predisposition all had main effects on later illness, although prior illness was controlled for statistically. The results from the analysis of variance indicated that stressful life events and constitutional predisposition increase illness, whereas personality-based hardiness decreases illness.

Kobasa et al. (1982) employed a research design to further test the effects of the hardy personality on the stress–illness link, using a sample of 259 male participants from the same utility company. Stress and illness were measured as in the earlier investigation. Six instruments were used to assess hardiness. They included two tests of commitment, the Alienation from Self and Alienation from Work scales from the Alienation Test (Maddi et al., 1979); two tests of control, the External Locus of Control Scale (Rotter, 1966) and the Powerlessness Scale of the Alienation Test (Maddi et al., 1979); and two tests of challenge, the Security Scale of the California Life Goals Evaluation Schedule (Hahn, 1969) and the Cognitive Structure Scale of the Personality Research Form (Jackson, 1974). The participants had to fill out the stress and illness questionnaires once a year for 3 years. The hardiness questionnaires were completed only in the first year.

As part of their analysis of the data, Kobasa et al. (1982) first examined information on the relationships among the six instruments used to measure hardiness. Inspection of the inter-correlation of the six scales prompted the removal of the Cognitive Structure questionnaire from the overall test. This resulted in the final use of five instruments to assess hardiness.

Further analyses of the data using an analysis of covariance with prior illness (measured in the first year) as the covariate, illness (measured in the second and third years) as the dependent variable, and hardiness (measured in the first year), and stress (measured in the second and third years) as independent variables indicated that stressful life events were associated with increased illness and that hardiness decreased the likelihood of symptom onset. Furthermore, hardiness interacted with stressful life events, indicating that it is especially important to be hardy if one is experiencing intensely stressful life events.

Kobasa et al. (1982) investigated the effects of hardiness and exercise as independent buffers in the stress–illness relationship. Self-report measures of exercise, hardiness, stressful events, and illness were obtained from 137 male business executives. Hardiness and exercise each interact with stressful events in decreasing illness. The participants who were high in both hardiness and exercise remained healthier than those high in one or the other only. These additive effects are consistent with the view that hardiness buffers by transforming the events themselves so as to decrease their stressfulness, whereas exercise acts as a buffer by decreasing the organismic strain resulting from experiencing stressful events.

Kobasa and Puccetti (1983) examined personality hardiness, social assets, and perceived social support as moderators of the effects of stressful life events on illness onset in a group of 170 middle- and upper level male executives (aged 32–65). Personality hardiness (assessed by three scales of the Alienation Test, the Security scale of the California Life Goals Evaluation Schedule, and Rotter's Internal-External Locus of Control Scale) and stressful life events (an adaptation of the Schedule of Recent Events) consistently influenced illness scores: the former serving to lower symptomatology (Seriousness of Illness Survey), and the latter to increase it.

Subsequent studies based on Kobasa's theory of hardiness support the moderating effect of hardiness on stress and its adverse effects. One such study by Kathryn Tarolli Jager (1994) conforms to Kobasa's hypothesis that the higher the level of hardiness in nurses, the less likely one experiences burnout due to stress. The author explains that nurses can use hardiness as the best buffer against burnout by putting one's sense of commitment, one's capacity for taking control of one's life, and one's zest for meeting a challenge as opportunities and not threats.

P. T. Bartone, a well-known researcher in this field of study, has also examined the sources of stress for American forces deployed to Bosnia, the relation of stress to psychiatric symptoms and post-traumatic stress disorder, and the influence of personality hardiness as a stress moderator or buffer (1998). His study also confirmed the stress-buffering role of hardiness as it served to moderate the effects of pre-deployment stress on later general psychiatric symptoms. Similar findings were obtained in which hardiness acts as a moderator and protector against the ill effects of combat exposure stress on Gulf War soldiers (Bartone, 1993, 1999). Likewise, various other researches also support the mediating effect of hardiness on an individual's stressful life events (Wendt, 1982; Collins, 1991; Blgbee, 1992).

Kobasa's views and suggested ingredients of hardiness have been extensively investigated by researchers since its inception, but lately, a number of researchers have come up with different perspectives. Maddi (2004, 2006b), the most consistent and prolific scholar in this field, also views hardiness as a combination of three types of attitudes—commitment, control, and challenge—rather than as a personality disposition which facilitates resiliency under stress. Maddi, in his paper 'Hardiness: The Courage to Be Resilient' (2006a), opines that the three attitudes of hardiness constitute the courage and motivation to face and transform stressors rather than to deny or to catastrophise and to avoid or strike out against them and are especially essential in our changing, turbulent times (p. 306). Maddi further argues that if these three attitudes are strong, the resulting courage and motivation facilitate strategic functioning with hardy action patterns that have the moderating effect of building social support, carrying out problem-solving (or transformational) coping, and engaging in beneficial self-care (2006b, p. 161).

According to Maddi (2006a), hardy attitudes facilitate effective coping in that individuals use transformational coping (i.e. engaging in problem-solving) as opposed to regressive coping (i.e. engaging in denial). That hardiness relates more to the simultaneous use of transformational coping than with regressive coping was found by another research done by Maddi and Hightower (1999). Thus, individuals with higher levels of hardiness are more likely to possess effective coping skills such as emphasising action, planning, and positive reinterpretation of the situation as opposed to ineffective coping skills such as mental disengagement, behavioural disengagement, denial, or alcohol and drug use (Maddi and Khoshaba, 1994; Maddi and Hightower, 1999).

While acknowledging the importance of the three core dimensions, Bartone et al. (2006) considered hardiness as something more global than mere attitudes. They conceive of hardiness as a broad personality style or generalised mode of functioning that includes cognitive, emotional, and behavioural qualities. This generalised style of functioning, which incorporates commitment, control, and challenge, is believed to affect how one views oneself and interacts with the world around them.

2.6 Kobasa's 3Cs of Hardiness

Derived theoretically from an existential psychology background, the hardiness construct is comprised of three interrelated, but separate, components of commitment, control, and challenge (Kobasa, 1979a; Maddi and Kobasa, 1984; Maddi, 2006a).

Commitment is the ability to find meaning and fulfilment during a stressful encounter (Kobasa, 1979a; Kobasa et al., 1982). Control is the belief that one influences the outcome of a stressful encounter no matter how many obstacles block one's path (Kobasa, 1979a; Kobasa et al., 1982). Challenge is the ability to view change as a normal part of life instead of as a threatening encounter (Kobasa, 1979a; Maddi and Kobasa, 1984). Whether a stressful experience is positive or negative, hardy individuals view the situation as a learning experience (Maddi and Khoshaba, 2005). In *Hardiness: Turning Stressful Circumstances Into Resilient Growth* (2013), Maddi re-asserts that

> conceptually, all three Cs of hardy attitudes need to be strong, in order to provide the existential courage and motivation to do the hard work of turning stresses to advantage; that hard work involves hardy coping, hardy social interaction, and hardy self-care.
>
> (p. 9)

The 3Cs of hardiness have been put forward as the pathway to resilience under stress (Bonanno, 2004; Maddi and Khoshaba, 2005). Resilience is seen as the phenomenon of maintaining our performance and health despite the occurrence of stressful circumstances. Maddi emphasises that resilience should also be considered to involve not only survival but thriving as well—in the sense that stressful circumstances can also enhance performance and health, through what we learn and then use. Thus, the combination of strong hardiness attitudes and strategies will result in the best possible living in our turbulent times (Maddi, 2013).

The general proposition that certain individuals may undergo psychological growth after stressful life events and that there exists individual differences in personality as a possible mediating factor in the stress–growth relationship was studied by Nemiroffin in his dissertation (1986). Multiple regression analyses of longitudinal questionnaire data which were collected from two samples of executive- and craft-level business managers who had participated in the study revealed that hardiness and life stress significantly predicted the increase in coping ability among the executives. Family stress and the commitment component of hardiness were also found to be important for psychological growth.

Another study which examined the relationship between the 3Cs and the experience of physical and psychological symptoms in adolescents was done by Shepperd and Kashani (1991) which found that low-stress men experienced few physical and psychological symptoms regardless of their levels of commitment and control, whereas high-stress men experienced more problems when they were low, rather than high, in either commitment or control. The hardiness components did not interact with stress in the prediction of health outcomes among women.

One of the first gender-sensitive studies on hardiness and its components based on only women subjects was done by Judith D. Fair (1993), in which she hypothesised that the high-stress/low-illness group, compared to their high-stress/high-illness counterparts, would (a) demonstrate a challenge disposition illustrated by greater optimism and by less emphasis on either an affiliation or achievement orientation; (b) be more committed to self, family, work, interpersonal relations, and social institutions; and (c) make greater use of control mechanisms through problem- and emotion-focused coping rather than regressive-focused coping. Results indicated that all the hypotheses were not confirmed, with a partial exception on the control dimension.

In a study on undergraduate college students done for his dissertation, Lynch (1995) examined the relationship among the commitment and control dimensions of hardiness, negative life events, and explanatory style. Attempts were also made to clarify the relationship between two widely, but predominantly separately, researched theories of cognitive coping styles of hardiness and reformulated learned helplessness (Abramson et al., 1978). Hierarchical and simultaneous multiple regression analyses showed that only commitment significantly increased the variance accounted for in explanatory style. The finding that commitment was correlated with an explanatory style but control was not provides support for the idea that hardiness and reformulated learned helplessness theories describe overlapping, but also distinct, constructs.

Bartone et al. (2009) found the 3Cs of Kobasa as having a broader application for leadership success in different situational contexts. The results of their study on army cadets provided an overall interesting profile of the generally effective leader as competent and committed, confident in their ability to manage events and influence outcomes, and conscientious, persistent, and savvy in the face of complex and changing conditions. Besides, this leader also has good insights into social relationships and the interface of individuals with social systems and organisations (social judgement).

In yet another study, Bartone (2013) presented a new taxonomy for organising and thinking about the multitude of factors associated with suicide in the military. He presented a model in which military-specific formative factors are shown to contribute to alienation and powerlessness: key factors that can lead to suicide. Drawing from the hardiness model of resilience, some recommendations were also provided for building a sense of commitment (vs. alienation) and control (vs. powerlessness) in military personnel as a strategy for reducing suicide.

Harrison and Brower (2011) made one of the first studies on the relationship with and impact of psychological hardiness (PH) on homesickness and cultural intelligence with 537 students (from a small private university in the southeastern United States) studying abroad. Results from a correlation analysis demonstrated a strong positive relationship between PH and psychological adjustment, as predicted, but the control dimension of PH was not related to homesickness. The strongest correlation was found between the challenge dimension of PH and homesickness. The commitment dimension of PH was correlated with homesickness but did not indicate a relationship using the median split procedure. So whether or not students embraced the new culture and actively involved themselves in it did not impact their degree of psychological adjustment. Furthermore, the combined effects of cultural intelligence (CQ) on PH showed no difference between having low measures of both CQ and PH and being strong in only one of these. Thus, the researchers concluded by saying that the impact of either CQ or PH is significant only in the presence of each other; that is they work together to create someone who better adjusts to the cross-cultural environment.

2.7 Hardiness and Culture

It has been a long time since Kobasa explored hardiness and its 3Cs as components of one's personality disposition. Since then, factors like globalisation, corporatisation, liberalisation, and the information technology (IT) revolution have significantly changed the world around us. The ways we look at work, family, society, and life in general have undergone a seachange. Therefore, it is now necessary to re-evaluate the extant principles and seek new dimensions of strategies for coping with stress under the umbrella of hardiness. Keeping in view these changes at workplaces all over the world, we need to explore the possibility of the presence of another trait (or traits) which could as well be looked at as components of hardiness. The study of such a perspective would be of immense value insofar as the stress coping of Indian corporate professionals is concerned.

We have a good number of studies and researches on hardiness focusing mostly on subjects pertaining to countries other than India. One particular aspect which called to my curiosity was the possible buffering role played by the typical cultural upbringing by Indians. Hypothetically, there is something special about the upbringing in Indian culture which equips one with intrinsic traits to encounter stress.

Needless to say, like any other country, India has its cultural traditions. More important, India has had a long and well-established culture built on the sturdy edifice of the country's rich heritage of literature, religion, philosophy, and value systems. Its multiculturalism has given it an assimilative but individual quality which is rarely seen elsewhere. In other words, Indians inherit not only a different culture but, in a sense, a unique one as well.

That culture is partly acquired and partly learned, is evident from the works of a number of scholars and researchers. There have been some studies on the effect of one's culture on personality vis-à-vis occupational stress and coping strategies. Some scholars and researchers have noticed significant differences in the stress level and coping mechanisms of professionals coming out of different cultures (Cohen et al., 1985; Etzion and Pines, 1986). Hofstede (1980) has reported that India presents a sharp contrast to the United States in two significant dimensions of values: individualism and power distance.

In *Psychological Stress and the Coping Process*, Lazarus (1966) submits that "[o]ften, individuals exposed to [a] threatening situation will make efforts to increase interpersonal contacts in an attempt to mobilize social resources" (p. 108). Hofstede (1983) has also indicated that individualism–CT was the major construct between Eastern and Western societies. CT, said to be a distinctive cultural trait of India, has been defined by Kapoor et al. (2003) as "a set of feelings, beliefs, behavioural intentions, and behaviours related to solidarity, concern for others, cooperation among members of in-group and the desire to develop a feeling of groupness with other members" (p. 687). Similarly, a significant difference has been found in the perception of the source of occupational stress by examining a sample of female clerical employees from an Eastern (i.e. India) and a Western (i.e. the United States) culture (Narayanan et al., 1999).

Hardiness can also be learnt or acquired in spite of it being considered as a personality disposition:

> The view that hardiness can be increased or decreased by life experiences does not signify that it must be other than a personality disposition. In all fully elaborated personality theories, there are some components that are present at birth, and others that develop through the interaction of the person with others and situations. There are many conceptualized personality dispositions (e.g., need for achievement, ego-strength, optimism, hardiness) that fit into this latter, developed category.
>
> (Maddi and Harvey, 2005, p. 418)

In *Resilience at Work: How to Succeed No Matter What Life Throws at You*, Maddi and Khoshaba (2005) describe how hardiness can be inculcated in individuals by proper training. They inform that their training at Illinois Bell Telephone (IBT) was effective in helping trainees learn hardy coping, social interaction, and attitudes (p. 56). According to the authors, resilience can be learned in childhood and that hardiness is often the outcome of family and social support. From their interaction with hardy individuals, they found that their parents supported these youngsters' capabilities through either encouraging their gifts and talents or assigning them family responsibilities or both. In their school, similarly, teachers or other adults spotted and nurtured these youngsters (p. 52).

Thus, from the previously discussed findings, we can say that theoretically, a sound background of culture can act as a strong foundation and help in the contribution of formation of personality. However, the role of Indian culture in the shaping of an individual's personality, hardy or otherwise, has not been adequately or convincingly studied.

2.8 The Measurement of Hardiness

In her introductory study on hardiness, Kobasa (1979a) had designed a composite questionnaire of 53 items to test the concept of personality hardiness and its three main components: control, commitment, and challenge. Overall, 18 variables were studied which were a result of the different aspects of each component of hardiness. It contained 19 different scales and was a composite questionnaire, made up of all or parts of five standardised instruments (Funk, 1992):

1. The Alienation Test (Maddi et al., 1979)—nine scales
2. The Personality Research Form (Jackson, 1974; Stricker, 1973; Wiggins, 1973)—four scales
3. The Internal–External Locus of Control Scale (Lefcourt, 1973, 1976; Rotter et al., 1962)
4. The California Life Goals Evaluation Schedules (Hahn, 1966)—three scales
5. The Role Consistency Test

Funk, in his 1992 review of hardiness, outlined changes that occurred to the original instrument, resulting in the retention of only five scales on "an inventory of 71 items that became the most widely used measure of hardiness—the Unabridged Hardiness Scale (UHS)" (p. 336). Funk also described the two short forms that followed the original measure, the 20-item Abridged Hardiness Scale (AHS) and the 36-item Revised Hardiness Scale (RHS), both of which appeared in 1982. Both the scales yielded an overall measure of hardiness like the original. Furthermore, it also yielded measures for the three facets of hardiness: control, commitment, and challenge.

The 36-item RHS, developed by Kobasa et al. (1982), was a result of a prospective design to test the hardiness scale and study the effects of the hardy personality on the stress–illness link. They used a sample of 259 male subjects from the same public utility company as in the earlier study of Kobasa. Stress and illness were measured as in the earlier investigation and six instruments were used to assess hardiness. The six subscales included two tests of commitment: the Alienation from Self and Alienation from Work scales from the Alienation Test (Maddi et al., 1979); two tests of control: the External Locus of Control Scale (Rotter et al., 1962) and the Powerlessness Scale of the Alienation Test (Maddi et al., 1979); and two tests of challenge: the Cognitive Structure Scale of the Personality Research Form (Jackson, 1974) and the Security Scale of the California Life Goals Evaluation Schedule (Hahn, 1966). In a check of internal consistency, it was found that Subscale 5 (Cognitive Structure) had either no correlation or was negatively correlated with the other subscales. The Cronbach's alpha (using subscale scores as items) increased from .59 to .73 when Subscale 5 was deleted. This prompted the removal of the Cognitive Structure questionnaire from the overall test and resulted in the final use of five instruments to assess hardiness.

This was consistent with more hardiness studies in which the Cognitive Structure subscale was not included in formulating an overall hardiness score (Kobasa et al., 1982; Kobasa et al., 1983; Kobasa and Puccetti, 1983; Kobasa et al., 1985; Wiebe and McCallum, 1986). Kobasa (1982b) stated that the revised scale correlated with the full scale at .89 and that all major findings were replicated when this scale was substituted for the full scale in her earlier samples.

While administering the scale on different subjects with different requirements, Kobasa developed a 50-item Personal Views Survey (PVS; Hardiness Institute, 1985) which was later modified to many other versions like 30 items of the PVS-II (Maddi, 1997), the PVS-III, and the PVS-III-Revised (PVS-III-R) (Maddi et al., 2009). The PVS-II included only items written specifically for relevance to hardiness (rather than incorporating scales already in use for other purposes) and used close to an equal number of positively and negatively worded items for the components of commitment, control, and challenge. The PVS-III-R is a revised version of PVS-II that includes 18 positively and negatively phrased items regarding the attitudes of commitment, control, and challenge that are combined in a composite score of overall hardiness. These 18 items were the most reliable and valid items that have survived from the PVS-II (Maddi and Khoshaba, 2001b). The PVS-III-R had an internal consistency reliability estimate of 0.81. Like most of its predecessors, the PVS-III measures the three subdimensions of hardiness: commitment, control, and challenge. The PVS-III can be administered independently, but it is also contained in a 106-item Hardi-Survey (Maddi and Khoshaba, 2001a) which "measures not only Hardy Attitudes, but other resistance resources of Work Support, Family Support, and Hardy Coping, along with the vulnerability factors of Stress, Strain, and Regressive Coping" (qtd. in O'Neal, 1999, p. 3). The inventory yields scores for Commitment, Control, and Challenge, as well as Total Hardiness. By now, the PVS-II and PVS-III-R have been translated into 16 European, Asian, and Middle Eastern languages. These translations are used around the world, to say nothing of the countries that use the original English versions (Maddi and Harvey, 2005).

Since the development of the 53-items hardiness scale by Kobasa in 1979, a bulk of hardiness research has been unfortunately limited to white-collar and managerial groups, such as executives, lawyers, and army officers (Kobasa, 1979a, 1981, 1982a; Maddi, 1987; Kobasa et al., 1981, 1982). The sample chosen for these studies mostly included male subjects. Thus, it rather appeared like a scale tailored for 'White male Americans' only.

A significant change brought about by Bartone (1984) extended the investigation on the measure of hardiness further when he constructed a scale specifically for blue-collar workers. The subjects of his study were 798 Chicago Transit Authority bus drivers (men and women) who were administered a 50-item blue-collar measure of hardiness that contained 20 commitment items (alpha = .89), 20 control items (alpha = .78), and 10 challenge items (alpha = .71). The overall reliability coefficient was found to be 0.90 for this 50-item scale. Because there were half as many items in the Challenge scale as in the other two scales, Challenge was given double weight in the Hardiness Composite Score. This scale was named by Bartone as the DRS.

With additional psychometric refinement, considering military samples led to an improved 45-item version (Bartone et al., 1989) and then a 30-item version (Bartone, 1991). Subsequently, a carefully conducted item and reliability analysis with mixed-gender military samples has resulted in a 15-item measure (DRS-15) that displays good psychometric properties and good evidence for the validity of the instrument as a measure of the hardiness construct (Bartone, 1995). The DRS-15 displayed excellent psychometric properties including Cronbach's alpha coefficients ranging from .70 to .77 (for the three sub-dimensions of control, commitment, and challenge) to .83 for the overall scale. However, the test-retest reliability was not estimated for the same until Bartone addressed the issue in 2007 by using a sample of military academy cadets. The 3-week test-retest reliability coefficient was 0.78, which indicates a high reliability.

By applying the principles of testing and international standards for test adaptation, the knowledge of the hardiness-resilience construct and knowledge of Norwegian language and culture, the DRS-15 scale was translated into Norwegian in 1998. It has since been used in multiple studies in Norway (Johnsen et al., 2004; Bartone et al., 2002). While most of the DRS-15 items appeared to be operating similarly in the Norwegian and American

versions, five items show some evidence of DIF—differential item functioning (Bartone et al., 2006, 2007). These results were applied to form a
new revision of the Norwegian DRS-15 hardiness scale, and have also led
to improvements in the original English language DRS-15 scale. Although
Bartone et al. (2007) claim that the results have been positive, there is evidence that the measure is in need of psychometric improvement in order
to capture the concept of hardiness more effectively in the Norwegian language and culture (Johnsen et al., 2004).

An Italian version was administered to a non-clinical sample of adults
($N = 150$), along with measures of psychological well-being (PWB-18) and
health. A subsample ($N = 66$) completed the DRS-15 again 1 month later.
Results showed good reliability in terms of internal consistency and test-
retest stability. With regard to the subscales, stability was high for all three
subscales, whereas two subscales (Commitment and Control) showed mar-
ginal internal consistency (Picardi et al., 2012).

C-DRS-15, the Chinese version, a result of the adaptation of an international
standard of cross-cultural translation and validation of patient-reported outcome measures, is among the first to confirm that the C-DRS-15, with modified factor structure from the original English DRS-15, is a reliable and valid
measurement tool to evaluate hardiness in Chinese women (Wong et al., 2014).

However, a few studies on DRS-15 have raised concern on the measurement equivalence of the construct of hardiness across gender.

2.9 Hardiness and Gender

From the previously discussed studies and investigations by various researchers, it is quite evident that hardiness and its three main components exert a
moderating effect between stress and its adverse outcomes. But many of these
studies have neglected a very important variable, gender, even though it has
been suggested to have differential effects in the stress–illness–resistance literature (Aneshensel and Pearlin, 1987; Braiker, 1986; Cleary, 1987; Lazarus
and Folkman, 1984; Miller, 2012).

Initially, hardiness was mostly studied on male subjects, neglecting
the women's mediating effects on stress–illness–hardiness relationships
(Kobasa, 1982a; Kobasa et al., 1981; Kobasa et al., 1982). Moreover, results
obtained from studies of men have been generalised as outcomes for women.
In the 1980s, researchers went for the first studies on the buffering effects
of hardiness in female participants (Ganellan and Blaney, 1984; Gentry and
Kobasa, 1984; Rhodewalt and Agustsdottir, 1984) that later became a source
of debate in hardiness studies.

An exceptional study which used only female participants was done by
Judith D. Fair (1993), who intended to have an exploratory investigation

of women and stress from a gender-sensitive perspective within the meta-construct of personality hardiness, an approach which had not been previously undertaken. Other studies that involved women participants provided mixed results only: Significant buffering effects have been found in some studies of illness outcomes (Rhodewalt and Zone, 1989) but not in the others (Schmied and Lawler, 1986).

Many other similar studies by few scholars have also yielded mixed results when they integrated the female gender as a specific variable, used diverse definitions of stress, and included various methodologies and different outcome measures (Pearlin and Schooler, 1978; Rich and Rich, 1987; Foster and Dion, 2003).

Hystad (2012) examined the measurement equivalence across gender in DRS-15. A multi-group confirmatory factor analytic approach revealed non-equivalence related to the Control subscale. However, follow-up analyses examining gender bias in the two non-equivalent items showed that the effect of gender was minimal. The gender effects found indicated that women had a greater tendency to endorse these items compared to men.

A moderate life stress–illness relationship which was stronger for women than for men was also studied by Claypoole (1987). However, there were no main effects indicating that hardiness functioned in a health-buffering fashion. Some gender differences were found in the relationship among hardiness, optimism, pessimism, engaged coping, disengaged coping, and the self-reported health measures by Stokes-Crowe (1998). Yet other research supports the finding that women have a significantly higher hardiness when compared to men in a study intended to explore the role of personality hardiness as a stress-resistance resource for male and female freshmen cadets at West Point (Bartone and Priest, 2001).

In contrast, several researchers have suggested that hardiness exerts weaker effects among women than among men (Holahan and Moos, 1985; Schmied and Lawler, 1986). Wiebe's (1991) study indicates that high-hardy men responded more adaptively to a laboratory stressor than did low-hardy men and that hardiness exerted either weaker or no effects among women. A similar study was done by Sanford (1991) to assess the effects of gender to the moderating effects of hardiness on physiological reactivity to two types of laboratory stressors, but the results indicated limited support for the moderating effects of hardiness, particularly for women.

Around the same time, Shepperd and Kashani (1991) examined the relationship between the hardiness components and the experience of physical and psychological symptoms in 75 male and 75 female adolescents and came up with similar findings. The most important finding was a consistent interaction of stress, gender, and hardiness for several of the health measures. The low-stress men experienced few physical and psychological symptoms regardless of their levels of commitment and control, and high-stress men experienced more problems when they were low rather than high in either commitment or control. The hardiness components did not interact with stress in the prediction of health outcomes among women.

Similarly, a significant finding of Klag and Bradley's study (2004) was that hardiness moderated the effects of stress on illness in men but not in women. The effect was demonstrated prospectively, using the composite scale and each of its subscales after controlling for neuroticism and occupation.

Apparently, findings obtained from the previous studies could not be taken as conclusive; therefore, gender differences in hardiness effects posed a major threat to the conceptualisation of the hardiness construct and pointed at a major problem in the methodology.

2.10 Hardiness and Demographic Factors

In the original IBT study of working adults, there were no differences in hardiness observed across the demographic variables of age, gender, mana-gerial rank, or ethnicity (Maddi and Kobasa, 1984). A few earlier studies had similar findings in which subjects did not show any significant differ-ence or relationship between age and hardiness (Kobasa, 1979a; Kobasa et al., 1981; Rhodewalt and Zone, 1989; Carson, 1990; Kelly, 1997; Han-sen, 2000).

However, a remarkable study by Maddi et al. (2006) on 1,239 partici-pants ranging in age from 17 to 85, belonging to lower to upper classes socio-economic statuses, and having education from the high school level to advanced degrees revealed a positive relationship between hardiness and its components with age. Likewise, the outcomes of a study by Parkes and Rendall (1988) also indicated that age accounted for a major variance in the hardiness scores, especially the different facets of hardiness when the researchers applied multiple regression analysis to the scores of the subjects.

Specific findings related to commitment—a facet of hardiness—in rela-tion to age originates from a study done by Sandhu et al. (2009), who found significant differences observed on the dimension of commitment of the Indian coaches on the basis of their age.

More confounding results were obtained from studies related to the hardi-ness and tenure of the subjects. The initial studies done by Kobasa and her associates revealed no relationship or significance between hardiness and ten-ure in a job. However, there are a few studies that have indicated a low correla-tion when hardiness and its sub-components were measured with the subjects' tenure in their current job (Dillard, 1990; Virgin, 1994). It was interesting to find a positive and meaningful correlation between hardiness and tenure from

Jana Radisic's study (2005), which found that police officers exhibited more hardiness and fewer total stressors as the tenure in their job increased.

As mentioned earlier, the first few studies done by Kobasa or her contemporaries and associates revealed no significant difference between hardiness and its components in relation to the levels of seniority/management (Kobasa, 1979a; Kobasa et al., 1981). Similarly, very low correlations and no significant relationships were found between job level and the subscales of hardiness in a later study done by Dillard (1990).

2.11 Conclusion

It is evident from the literature review that although there is a considerable corpus of studies on stress, personality types, and hardiness on the parameters of gender, age, hierarchy, and the like, there has not been enough focus on the Indian situation.

India is basically a country with an ancient value system arising from its cultural traditions which are more or less governed by spiritual principles. The age-old Sanatana Dharma has undergone a benign synthesis after coming in contact with the other creeds like Islam, Christianity, and Zoroastrianism which came into the country. The various religious and reform movements, as well as the founding of religious belief systems evolving out of the country itself, such as Buddhism, Jainism, and Sikhism, among others, and the belief systems of the ethnic communities have also contributed immensely to the essential Indian culture and value systems.

Indian culture has come into collision with several external influences but has always assimilated them in a benign manner. However, after globalisation and the advent of the internet, as well as corporate economics, India has been exposed to a hitherto unprecedented kind of life, especially for those who are employed by corporate houses or even start-ups. Needless to say, the situation has become quite challenging for the Indian professionals, but there has hardly been any study to assess their levels of stress, their coping ability, and the efficacy of their cultural upbringing in negotiating their job and life stressors.

References

Abramson, L. Y., Seligman, M. E. P., and Teasdale, J. D. (1978). Learned helplessness in humans: Critique and reformulation. *Journal of Abnormal Psychology*, *87*(1), 49–74. DOI: 10.1037/0021-843X.87.1.49

Aneshensel, C. S., and Pearlin, L. I. (1987). Structural contexts of sex differences in stress. In R. C. Barnett, L. Biener, and G. K. Baruch (Eds.), *Gender and stress* (pp. 75–95). Free Press.

Antonovsky, A. (1979). *Health, stress and coping*. Jossey-Bass.

Asbell, L. (1988). Style of coping, daily hassles, and hardiness as mediators and outcomes in the stress-illness relationship: A prospective study. Dissertation, Washington State University. UMI, Ann Arbor, USA. asbellhealth.com› wp-content › uploads › 2018/05 › VITA-05182018

Bartone, P. T. (1984). Stress and health in Chicago Transit Authority bus drivers. Dissertation, Department of Behavioral Sciences, University of Chicago.

Bartone, P. T. (1991). Development and validation of a short hardiness measure. Paper presented at the Third Annual Convention of the American Psychological Society, Washington, DC. www.hardiness-resilience.com

Bartone, P. T. (1993). Psychosocial predictors of soldier adjustment to combat stress. Paper presented at the Third European Conference on Traumatic Stress, Bergen, Norway. www.hardiness-resilience.com

Bartone, P. T. (1995). A short hardiness scale. Paper presented at the American Psychological Society Annual Convention, New York. www.hardiness-resilience.com

Bartone, P. T. (August 1998). Stress, hardiness & symptoms in Bosnia deployed soldiers. Paper presented at the American Psychological Association Convention, San Francisco. www.hardiness-resilience.com/docs/APA98.pdf

Bartone, P. T. (1999). Hardiness protects against war-related stress in Army Reserve Forces. *Consulting Psychology Journal: Practice and Research, 51*(2), 72–82.

Bartone, P. T. (2007). Test-retest reliability of the dispositional resilience scale-15: A brief hardiness scale. *Psychological Reports, 101*, 943–944. www.hardiness-resilience.com

Bartone, P. T. (2013). A new taxonomy for understanding factors leading to suicide in the military. *International Journal of Emergency Mental Health and Human Resilience*, Chevron Publishing, *15*(4), 299–306.

Bartone, P. T., Eid, J., Johnsen, B. H., Laberg, J. C., Saus, E. R., and Hystad, S. (2007). Cross-cultural adaptation of the DRS-15 dispositional resilience scale (psychological hardiness). Paper presented at the American Psychological Association Annual Convention, San Francisco. www.hardiness-resilience.com/docs/Bartone-etal-2007-APA-SF.pdf

Bartone, P. T., Johnsen, B. H., Eid, J., Brun, W., and Laberg, J. C. (2002). Factors influencing small-unit cohesion in Norwegian navy officer cadets. *Military Psychology, 14*(1), 1–22.

Bartone, P. T., Johnsen, B. H., Eid, J., Laberg, J. C., and Snook, S. A. (2009). Big five personality factors, hardiness, and social judgment as predictors of leader performance. *Leadership and Organizational Development Journal, 30*(6), 498–521. http://dx.doi.org/10.1108/01437730910981908l

Bartone, P. T., Johnsen, B. H., Eid, J., Laberg, J. C., Thayer, J., and Sommerfeldt-Pettersen, J. (7 November 2006). International adaptation of a brief human resiliency (hardiness) scale. Presented at the Association of Military Surgeons of the U.S (AMSUS) Annual Meeting, San Antonio, Texas. www.researchgate.net/publication/

228509154_International_adaptation_of_a_brief_human_resiliency_hardiness_scale/link/02bfe5141d35b1c609000000/download

Bartone, P. T., Johnsen, B. H., Eid, J., Molde, H., Hystad, S., and Laberg, J. C. (2007). DIF: Differential item functioning analysis of Norwegian and American hardiness measures. Paper presented at the Association for Psychological Science Annual Convention, Washington, DC. www.hardiness-resilience.com/docs/bartone-APS-handout.pdf

Bartone, P. T., and Priest, R. F. (2001). Sex differences in hardiness and health among West point cadets. Paper Presented at the 13th Annual Convention of the American Psychological Society, Toronto. www.hardiness-resilience.com

Bartone, P. T., Ursano, R. J., Wright, K. M., and Ingraham, L. H. (1989). The impact of a military air disaster on the health of assistance workers: A prospective study. *Journal of Nervous & Mental disease*, *177*(6), 317–328.

Bell, R. A., LeRoy, J. B., and Stephenson, J. J. (1982). Evaluating the mediating effects of social support upon life events and depressive symptoms. *Journal of Community Psychology*, *10*(4), 325–340. https://doi.org/10.1002/1520-6629(198210)10:4<325::AIDJCOP2290100405>3.0.CO;2-C

Blatny, M., and Adam, Z. (2008). Type C personality (cancer personality): Current view and implications for future research [in Czech]. *Vnitr Lek*, *54*(6), 638–645.

Blgbee, J. L. (1992). Family stress, hardiness and illness: A pilot study. *Family Relations, National Council on Family Relations*, *41*, 212–217. www.jstor.org/stable/584835

Bonanno, G. (2004). Loss, trauma, and human resilience: How we underestimated the human capacity to thrive after extremely aversive events. *American Psychologist*, *51*, 72–82.

Braiker, H. B. (1986). *The type E women: How to overcome the stress of being everything to everybody*. Signet.

Brown, G. W., Bhrolchain, M. Ni, and Harris, T. (1975). Social class and psychiatric disturbance among women in an urban population. *Sociology*, *9*(2), 225–254. https://doi.org/10.1177/003803857500900203

Brown, G. W., and Harris, T. (1978). *Social origins of depression: A study of psychiatric disorder in women*. Free Press.

Carson, V. B. (1990). The relationship of spiritual well-being, selected demographic variables, spiritual variables, health indicators, and AIDS related activities to hardiness in persons who were HIV + or were diagnosed with ARC or AIDS. Dissertation submitted to the University of Maryland for the degree of PhD. UMI, Ann Arbor, USA. Retrieved from ProQuest Digital Dissertations.

Claypoole, K. H. J. (1987). The impact of stressful life events on illness rates and immune functioning as moderated by type A behavior, hardiness, loneliness, nutrition, and exercise. Dissertation submitted to the Department of Psychology and the Graduate School of the University of Wyoming for the Degree of Doctor of Philosophy. UMI, Ann Arbor, USA. Retrieved from ProQuest Digital Dissertations.

Cleary, P. D. (1987). Gender differences in stress-related disorders. In R. C. Barnett, L. Biener, and G. K. Baruch (Eds.), *Gender and stress* (pp. 39–72). Free Press.

Cobb, S. (1976). Social support as moderator of life stress. *Psychosomatic Medicine*, *38*, 300–314.

Cohen, S., and Wills, T. A. (1985). Stress, social support, and the buffering hypothesis. *Psychological Bulletin*, *98*(2), 310–357. www.lchc.ucsd.edu/MCA/Mail/xmcamail. 2012_11.dir/pdfYukILvXsL0.pdf

Collins, C. B. (1991). Hardiness in adolescence: An enquiry into stress resistance. Dissertation, CUNY. UMI, Ann Arbor, USA. Retrieved from ProQuest Digital Dissertations.

Contrada, R. J. (1989). Type A behavior, personality hardiness, and cardiovascular responses to stress. *Journal of Personality and Social Psychology*, *57*(5), 895–903. DOI: 10.1037/0022-3514.57.5.895

De Jong, G. M., and Emmelkamp, P. M. (2000). Implementing a stress management training: Comparative trainer effectiveness. *Journal of Occupational Health Psychology*, *5*(2), 309–320.

DeLongis, A., and Holtzman, S. (2005). Coping in context: The role of stress, social support, and personality in coping. *Journal of Personality*, *73*(6), 1633–1656. https://doi.org/10.1111/j.1467-6494.2005.00361.x

Dillard, N. L. (1990). Hardiness and academic achievement. Dissertation submitted for the Doctor of Nursing Science Degree in the School of Nursing, Indiana University. UMI, Ann Arbour, USA. Retrieved from ProQuest Digital Dissertations.

Dohrenwend, B. S., and Dohrenwend, B. P. (Eds.) (1974). *Stressful life events: Their nature and effects*. Wiley and Sons.

Dohrenwend, B. S., & B. P. Dohrenwend (Eds.) (1984). *Stressful Life Events and their Contexts*. New Brunswick, New Jersey: Rutgers University Press.

Etzion, D., and Pines, A. (1986). Sex and culture in burnout and coping among human service professionals: A social psychological perspective. *Journal of Cross-Cultural Psychology*, *17*(2), 191–209. https://doi.org/10.1177/0022002186017002004

Fair, J. D. (1993). Personality hardiness: A gender-sensitive study of women and stress. Dissertation, Indiana University of Pennsylvania. UMI, Ann Arbour, USA. Retrieved from ProQuest Digital Dissertations.

Foster, M. D., and Dion, K. L. (2003). Dispositional hardiness and women's well-being relating to gender discrimination: The role of minimization. *Psychology of Women Quarterly*, *27*, 197–208.

Friedman, M., and Rosenman, R. (1974). *Type A behaviour and your heart*. Knopf.

Funk, S. C. (1992). Hardiness: A review of theory and research. *Health Psychology*, *11*, 335–345.

Ganellen, R. J., and Blaney, P. H. (1984). Hardiness and social support as moderators of the effects of life stress. *Journal of Personality and Social Psychology*, *47*, 156–163.

Gentry, W. D., and Kobasa, S. C. (1984). Social and psychological resources mediating stress-illness relationships in humans. In W. D. Gentry (Ed.), *Handbook of behavioural medicine* (pp. 87–116). Guilford Press.

Gore, S. (1978). The effect of social support in moderating the health consequences of unemployment. *Journal of Health and Social Behavior*, *19*(2), 157–165. DOI: 10.2307/2136531

Hahn, M. E. (1966). *California Life Goals Evaluation Schedules*. Palo Alto, Calif.: Western Psychological Services.

Hahn, M. E. (1969). *The California life goals evaluation schedule*. Western Psychological Press.

Hansen, C. (2000). Is there a relationship between hardiness and burnout in full-time staff nurses versus per diem nurses? *Masters Theses, 616*. https://scholarworks.gvsu.edu/theses/616

Hardiness Institute. (1985). Personal Views Survey. Arlington Heights, IL: Author

Harrison, J. K., and Brower, H. H. (Fall 2011). The impact of cultural intelligence and psychological hardiness on homesickness among study abroad students. *Frontiers: The Interdisciplinary Journal of Study Abroad, 21*, 41–62. https://files.eric.ed.gov/fulltext/EJ991042.pdf

Hinkle, L. E., Jr. (December 1974). The concept of "stress" in the biological and social sciences. *The International Journal of Psychiatry in Medicine, 5*(4), 335–357. https://doi.org/10.2190/91DK-NKAD-1XP0-Y4RG

Hofstede, G. (1980). *Culture's Consequences: International Differences in Work Related Values*. Sage Publications.

Hofstede, G. (December 1983). Culture's consequences: International differences in work-related values. *Administrative Science Quarterly, 28*(4), 625–629.

Holahan, C. J., and Moos, R. H. (1985). Life stress and health: Personality, coping, and family support in stress resistance. *Journal of Personality and Social Psychology, 49*(3), 739–747.

Holmes, T. H., and Masuda, M. (1974). Life change and illness susceptibility. In B. S. Dohrenwend and B. P. Dohrenwend (Eds.), *Stressful life events: Their nature and effects*. John Wiley & Sons. http://dx.doi.org/10.1037/1061-4087.51.2.95

Holmes, T. H., and Rahe, R. H. (1967). The social readjustment rating scale. *Journal of Psychosomatic Research, 11*(2), 213–218. https://doi.org/10.1016/0022-3999(67)90010-4

Hystad, S. W. (2012). Exploring gender equivalence and bias in a measure of psychological hardiness. *International Journal of Psychological Studies, 4*(4), 69–79.

Jackson, D. N. (1974). *Personality research form manual*. Research Psychologists Press.

Jager, K. T. (1994). Personal hardiness: Your buffer against burnout. *The American Journal of Nursing, 94*(2), 71–72.

Johnsen, B. H., Eid, J., and Bartone, P. T. (2004). Psykologisk "hardførhet": Kortversjonenav the short hardiness scale. *Tidsskrift for NorskPsykologforening, 41*, 476–477.

Kapoor, S., Hughes, P. C., Baldwin, J. R., and Blue, J. (2003). The relationship of individualism-collectivism and self-construals to communication styles in India and the United States. *International Journal of Intercultural Relations, 27*, 683–700. https://doi.org/10.1016/j.ijintrel.2003.08.002

Kelly, M. B. (1997). The effect of work-related and personal demographic variables on burnout and hardiness in nurse managers. A thesis proposal presented to The Facultyof the Department of Nursing, Clarkson College. UMI, Ann Arbor, USA. Retrieved from ProQuest Digital Dissertations.

Khoshaba, D. M., and Maddi, S. R. (2004). *HardiTraining: Managing stressful change* (5th ed.). Hardiness Institute.

Klag, S., and Graham, B. (2004). The role of hardiness in stress and illness: An exploration of the effect of negative affectivity and gender. *British Journal of Health Psychology, 9*, 137–161. DOI: 10.1348/135910704773891014

Kobasa, S. C. (January 1979a). Stressful life events, personality, and health: An inquiry into hardiness. *Journal of Personality and Social Psychology, 37*(1), 1–11.

Kobasa, S. C. (1981). Barriers to work stress: The hardy personality. In D. Gentry (Ed.), *Behavioral medicine: Work, stress, and health* (pp. 181–204). Martinus Nijhoff Publishers. https://books.google.co.in/books?id=LHehBQAAQBAJ&printsec=frontcover#v=onepage&q&f=false

Kobasa, S. C. (1982a). Commitment and coping in stress resistance among lawyers. *Journal of Personality and Social Psychology, 42*(4), 707–717. https://doi.org/10.1037/0022-3514.42.4.707

Kobasa, S. C. (1982b). The hardy personality: Toward a social psychology of stress and health. In G. Sanders and J. Suls (Eds.), *Social psychology of health and illness* (pp. 3–32). Erlbaum.

Kobasa, S. C., Maddi, S. R., and Courington, S. (1981). Personality and constitution as mediators in the stress-illness relationship. *Journal of Health and Social Behaviour, 22*, 368–378.

Kobasa, S. C., Maddi, S. R., and Kahn, S. (1982). Hardiness and health: A prospective study. *Journal of Personality and Social Psychology, 42*, 168–177. http://dx.doi.org/10.1037/0022-3514.42.1.168

Kobasa, S. C., Maddi, S. R., and Puccetti, M. C. (1982). Personality and exercise as buffers in the stress-illness relationship. *Journal of Behavioural Medicine, 5*, 391–404.

Kobasa, S. C., Maddi, S. R., Puccetti, M. C., and Zola, M. A. (1985). Effectiveness of hardiness, exercise and social support as resources against illness. *Journal of Psychosomatic Research, 29*, 525–533.

Kobasa, S. C., Maddi, S. R., and Zola, M. A. (1983). Type A and hardiness. *Journal of Behavioural Medicine, 6*, 41–51.

Kobasa, S. C., and Puccetti, M. C. (1983). Personality and social resources in stress-resistance. *Journal of Personality and Social Psychology, 45*, 839–850.

Lazarus, R. S. (1966). *Psychological stress and the coping process.* McGraw-Hill.

Lazarus, R. S., and Folkman, S. (1984). *Stress, appraisal and coping.* New York: Springer Publications.

Lazarus, R. S., and Launier, R. (1978). Stress-related transactions between person and environment. In L. A. Pervin and M. Lewis (Eds.), *Perspectives in interactional psychology* (pp. 287–327). Plenum.

Lefcourt, H. M. (1973). The function of the illusions of control and freedom. *American Psychologist, 28*(5), 417–425.

Lefcourt, H. M. (1976). *Locus of control: Current trends in theory and research.* Lawrence Erlbaum Associates.

Lynch, B. G. (1995). An examination of the relationship among the commitment and control dimensions of hardiness, the appraised impact and frequency of negative life events, and optimistic explanatory style. Dissertation, The University of

Tennessee, Knoxville. UMI, Ann Arbor, USA. Retrieved from ProQuest Digital Dissertations.

Lynch, J. J. (1977). *Broken heart: The medical consequences of loneliness.* Basic Books, Inc.

Maddi, S. R. (1987). Hardiness training at illinois bell telephone. In J. P. Opatz (Ed.), *Health promotion evaluation* (pp. 101–115). National Wellness Institute.

Maddi, S. R. (1990). Issues and interventions in stress mastery. In H. S. Friedman (Ed.), *Personality and disease* (pp. 121–154). Wiley.

Maddi, S. R. (1997). Personal views survey II: A measure of dispositional hardiness. In C. P. Zalaquett and R. J. Woods (Eds.), *Evaluating stress: A book of resources* (pp. 293–310). Scarecrow Education.

Maddi, S. R. (2002). The story of hardiness: Twenty years of theorizing, research and practice. *Consulting Psychology Journal: Practice and Research, 54*(3), 173–185.

Maddi, S. R. (2004). Hardiness: An operationalization of existential courage. *Journal of Humanistic Psychology, 44*(3), 279–298.

Maddi, S. R. (2006a). Hardiness: The courage to be resilient. In J. C. Thomas and D. L. Segal (Eds.), *Comprehensive handbook of personality and psychopathology: Personality and everyday functioning* (vol. 1, pp. 306–321). John Wiley & Sons.

Maddi, S. R. (2006b). Hardiness: The courage to grow from stresses. *The Journal of Positive Psychology: Dedicated to Furthering Research and Promoting Good Practice, 1*(3), 160–168. https://doi.org/10.1080/17439760600619609

Maddi, S. R. (2013). *Hardiness: Turning stressful circumstances into resilient growth.* Springer.

Maddi, S. R., and Harvey, R. H. (2005). Hardiness considered across cultures. In P. T. P. Wong and L. C. J. Wong (Eds.), *Handbook of multicultural perspectives on stress and coping* (pp. 409–426). Springer. https://doi.org/10.1007/0-387-26238-5_17

Maddi, S. R., Harvey, R. H., Khoshaba, D. M., Lu, J. L., Persico, M., and Brow, M. (2006). The personality construct of hardiness, III: Relationships with repression, innovativeness, authoritarianism, and performance.

Maddi, S. R., Harvey, R. H., Khoshaba, D. M., Fazel, M., and Resurreccion, N. (2009). The personality construct of hardiness, IV: Expressed in positive cognitions and emotions concerning oneself and developmentally relevant activities. *Journal of Humanistic Psychology, 49*(3), 292–305.

Maddi, S. R., and Hightower, M. (1999). Hardiness and optimism as expressed in coping patterns. *Consulting Psychology Journal: Practice and Research, 51*, 95–105.

Maddi, S. R., and Khoshaba, D. M. (1994). Hardiness and mental health. *Journal of Personality Assessment, 63*, 265–274. https://doi.org/10.1007/978-94-007-5222-1_1

Maddi, S. R., and Khoshaba, D. M. (2001a). *HardiSurvey III-R: Test development and instruction manual.* Hardiness Institute.

Maddi, S. R., and Khoshaba, D. M. (2001b). *Personal views survey III-R: Test development and internet instruction manual.* Hardiness Institute.

Maddi, S. R., and Khoshaba, D. M. (2005). *Resilience at work: How to succeed no matter what life throws at you.* American Management Association.

Maddi, S. R., and Kobasa, S. C. (1984). *The hardy executive: Health under stress.* Dow Jones-Irwin.

Maddi, S. R., Kobasa, S. C., and Hoover, M. (1979). The alienation test: A structured measure of a multidimensional subjective state. *Journal of Humanistic Psychology, 19*(4), 73–76.

Miller, J. B. (2012). *Toward a new psychology of women.* Beacon Press.

Narayanan, L., Menon, S., and Spector, P. E. (1999). Stress in the workplace: A comparison of gender and occupations. *Journal of Organizational Behavior, 20*(1), 63–73.

Nemiroff, D. G. (1986). Stressful life events, personality hardiness, and psychological growth. Dissertation, City University of New York. UMI, Ann Arbor, USA. Retrieved from ProQuest Digital Dissertations.

Nuckolls, K. B., Cassel, J., and Kaplan, B. H. (1972). Psychosocial assets, life crisis and the prognosis of pregnancy. *American Journal of Epidemiology, 95*, 431–441. https://doi.org/10.1017/CBO9780511759048.007

O'Neal, M. R. (17–19 November 1999). Measuring resilience. Paper presented at the Annual Meeting of the Mid-South Educational Research Association, Point Clear, AL. https://files.eric.ed.gov/fulltext/ED436574.pdf

Parkes, K. R., and Rendall, D. (1988). The hardy personality and its relationship to extraversion and neuroticism. *Journal of Personality and Individual Differences, 9*(4), 785–790.

Pearlin, L. I., and Schooler, C. (1978). The structure of coping. *Journal of Health and Social Behavior, 19*, 2–21.

Picardi, A., Bartone, P. T., et al. (2012). Development and validation of the Italian version of the 15-item dispositional resilience scale. *Rivista di psichiatria, 47*(3), 231–237.

Radisic, J. (2005). Police hardiness and officer's length of service. Dissertation Submitted to the Faculty of the Chicago School of Professional Psychology for the Degree of Doctor of Psychology. UMI, Ann Arbor, USA. Retrieved from ProQuest Digital Dissertations.

Rahe, R. H. (1974). The pathway between subjects' recent life change and their near-future illness reports: Representative results and methodological issues. In B. S. Dohrenwend and B. P. Dohrenwend (Eds.), *Stressful life events: Their nature and effects* (pp. 205–262). Wiley.

Rhodewalt, F., and Zone, J. B. (1989). Appraisal of life change, depression and illness in hardy and non-hardy women. *Journal of Personality and Social Psychology, 56*(1), 81–86.

Rhodewalt, R., and Agustsdottir, S. (1984). On the relationship of hardiness to the type A behavior pattern: Perception of life events verses coping with life events. *Journal of Research in Personality, 18*, 212–223.

Rich, V. L., and Rich, A. R. (1987). Personality hardiness and burnout in female staff nurses. *Image: Journal of Nursing Scholarship, 19*, 63–66.

Rotter, J. B. (1966). Generalized Expectancies for internal versus external control of reinforcement. *Psychological Monographs: General and Applied, 80*(1), 1–28. DOI: 10.1037/h0092976

Rotter, J. B., Seeman, M., and Liverant, S. (1962). Internal versus external control of reinforcement: A major variable in behaviour theory. In N. F. Washburne (Ed.), *Decisions, values, and groups* (vol. 2, pp. 473–516). Pergamum Press.

Sandhu, K. S., Sharma, R. K., and Singh, A. (2009). Personality hardiness of Indian coaches in relation to their age and coaching experience. *Journal of Exercise Science and Physiotherapy, 5*(1), 38–41.

Sanford, B. T. (1991). The effects of hardiness and gender on psychophysiological reactivity to two types of stressors. Dissertation, Texas A & M University. UMI, Ann Arbor, USA. Retrieved from ProQuest Digital Dissertations.

Schmeid, L. A., and Lawler, K. A. (1986). Hardiness, type A behavior, and the stress-illness reaction in working women. *Journal of Personality and Social Psychology, 51,* 1218–1223.

Shepperd, J. A., and Kashani, J. H. (1991). The relationship of hardiness, gender, and stress to health outcomes in adolescents. *Journal of Personality, 59*(4), 747–768. https://people.clas.ufl.edu/shepperd/files/Hardiness.pdf

Sher, L. (2005). Type D personality: The heart, stress, and cortisol. *QJM: An International Journal of Medicine, 98,* 323–329. DOI: 10.1093/qjmed/hci064

Stokes-Crowe, L. A. (1998). Hardiness, one of several personality constructs thought to affect health. Dissertation submitted to the Division of Research and Advanced Studies of the University of Cincinnati for the degree of Ph.D. in the Department of Psychology of the College of Arts and Sciences. UMI, Ann Arbor, USA. Retrieved from ProQuest Digital Dissertations.

Stricker, L. J. (March 1973). Personality research form: Factor structure and response style involvement. *Educational Testing Service.* https://onlinelibrary.wiley.com/doi/pdf/10.1002/j.2333-8504.1973.tb00460.x

Virgin, S. E. M. (1994). Perceived stress and hardiness in female deans of schools of nursing. Dissertation submitted for the degree of Doctor of Science in Nursing in the School of Nursing in the Graduate School, the University of Alabama at Birmingham. UMI, Ann Arbor, USA. Retrieved from ProQuest Digital Dissertations.

Wendt, B. R. (1982). The role of hardiness as a mediator between stress and illness among adolescents. Dissertation submitted to the University of San Francisco. UMI, Ann Arbor, USA. Retrieved from ProQuest Digital Dissertations.

Wiebe, D. J. (1991). Hardiness and stress moderation: A test of proposed mechanisms. *Journal of Personality and Social Psychology, 60*(1), 89–99. https://doi.org/10.1037/0022-3514.60.1.89

Wiebe, D. J., and McCallum, D. M. (1986). Health practices and hardiness as mediators in the stress-illness relationship. *Health Psychology, 5,* 425–438.

Wiggins, J. S. (1973). Personality structure. In P. R. Farnsworth (Ed.), *Annual Review of Psychology* (vol. 19, pp. 293–350). Annual Reviews.

Wong, J., Fong, D., Choi, A., Chan, C., Tiwari, A., Chan, K. L., Lai, V., Logan, T., and Bartone, P. (2014). Transcultural and psychometric validation of the Dispositional Resilience Scale (DRS-15) in Chinese adult women. *Quality of Life Research, 23,* 2489–2494. DOI: 10.1007/s11136-014-0713-9

Wyler, A. R., Masuda, M., and Holmes, T. H. (1970). The seriousness of illness rating scale: Reproducibility. *Journal of Psychosomatic Research, 14*(1), 59–64. https://doi.org/10.1016/0022-3999(70)90070-X

Zuckerman, M. (1971). Dimensions of sensation seeking. *Journal of Consulting and Clinical Psychology, 36*(1), 45–52.

3 Data Analysis and Interpretation

3.1 Introduction

The present research is about the relationship of stress with hardiness and assessing the efficacy of culture as another contributing factor in making hardy professionals. Several objectives were set to find out the relationships between the three major variables of this study—Role Stress, Hardiness, and Culture. The **first objective** of this study was to assess the relationship between hardiness and its three components (commitment, control, and challenge) with various role stresses among the Indian corporate professionals. The **second objective** of this study was to assess the impact of the socio-demographic factors of hardiness on corporate professionals, particularly emphasising the impact of gender and age of the professionals on their hardiness levels. The **third objective** was to assess whether the socio-demographic factors, particularly, gender, age, and marital status have any impact on the role stress of the corporate professionals. The **fourth objective** was to identify the various aspects of culture that have an impact on hardiness and that culture could also be considered as a vital component of hardiness in the Indian context. The **final objective** of this study was to assess whether there exists any significant variation between the levels of role stress, hardiness, and various facets of Indian culture, experienced by the corporate professionals with respect to two sectors—information technology (IT) and banking—and two cities—Bengaluru and Bhubaneswar—in this study.

Keeping in view the preceding objectives and the design of the research, a composite questionnaire comprising three different scales related to role stress, hardiness, and Indian culture was administered to the sample of this study. The sample was drawn based on a purposive sampling technique from a pool of Indian corporate professionals specifically working in the banking and IT sectors and living in Bengaluru and Bhubaneswar. The inclusion of these two sectors and cities has been done with the purpose of finding out the differences, if any exist, among the professionals coming from different cities and different sectors. A total of 320 professionals—160 from each sector—40 from each of the 8 companies (20 from each city) were emailed the composite questionnaire. **Figure 3.1** gives an impression of how the questionnaire was distributed across both the sectors and cities.

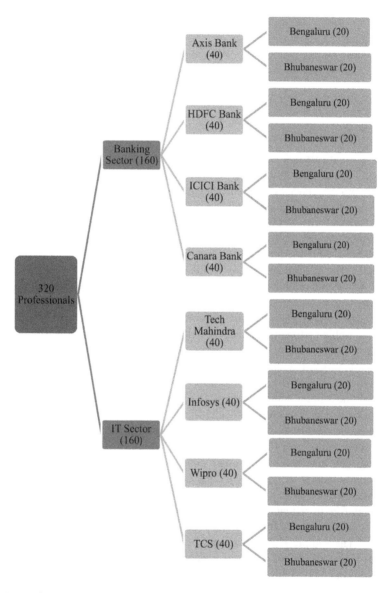

Figure 3.1 Distribution of Questionnaire Among 320 Professionals

After rejecting a few questionnaires due to errors and incomplete responses from the participants, the sample size came down to 234.

3.2 Sample Distribution

The sample size for the present study consisted of 234 corporate professionals, out of which 123 professionals belong to Bengaluru and 111 belong to Bhubaneswar. If the distribution based on sectors is looked at, there are 120 professionals from the banking sector and 114 from the IT sector. **Figure 3.2** depicts the sample obtained across sectors and cities.

The sample distribution across the two cities and sectors based on the socio-demographic factor—**Gender**—revealed that, out of 120 men, 54 professionals were from banking and 66 from IT. The total number of female professionals was 114, out of which 66 were from banking and 48 from IT. Out of 54 male bank professionals, 57.40% were from Bengaluru and 42.60% from Bhubaneswar, whereas it was 45.45% and 54.55%, respectively, for male IT professionals. The distribution was equal (50%) for both the cities for female bank professionals. Among the female professionals working in the IT sector, 60.42% were from Bengaluru and 39.58% from Bhubaneswar city. The distribution of the sample was fairly balanced by including an adequate number of respondents for all three variables.

The results related to the socio-demographic factor—**Age**—depicted that 56.52% of banking professionals for the age group 'Below 30 Years', were from Bengaluru and 43.48% from Bhubaneswar city, whereas for IT professionals, it was 57.9% and 42.1%, respectively. The percentage of professionals working in banking in the '30–40 Years' age group constituted about 48.39% from Bengaluru and 51.61% from Bhubaneswar city, whereas, it was 44.44% and 55.56%, respectively, for IT professionals. The age group of 'Above 40 Years' constituted about 66.67% from Bengaluru and 33.33%

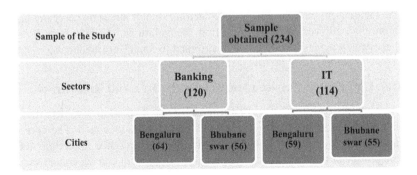

Figure 3.2 Sample Obtained Across Sectors and Cities

from Bhubaneswar city, whereas it was equally distributed for both the cities for professionals working in the IT sector. The distribution of the sample was fairly balanced by including an adequate number of respondents for all three variables.

The distribution of sample based on **Marital Status** across cities and sectors represented that 55.8% of the married bank professionals were from Bengaluru and 44.2% from Bhubaneswar city, whereas it was 45.83 % and 54.17%, respectively, for the married IT professionals. Among the bank professionals who were unmarried, 47.1% were from Bengaluru and 52.9% from Bhubaneswar city, whereas it was 62% and 38%, respectively, for the unmarried professionals working in the IT sector.

So far as the socio-demographic factor—**LOMs**—was concerned, 52.94% of senior banking professionals were from Bengaluru and 47.06% were from Bhubaneswar city, whereas it was 54.54% and 45.46%, respectively, for IT professionals. Among the bank professionals who were at the middle level, 53.85% were from Bengaluru and 46.15% from Bhubaneswar city, whereas it was 54.1% and 45.9%, respectively, for IT professionals. About 52% of the bank professionals at the junior level were from Bengaluru and 48% from Bhubaneswar city, whereas it was 45.16 % and 54.84%, respectively, for IT professionals.

The results related to the distribution of sample across cities and sectors in terms of **Tenure** in their current job showed that the banking professionals who have been serving in the company for less than a year constituted about 44% of those from Bengaluru and 56% from Bhubaneswar, whereas it was 42.86% and 57.14%, respectively, for IT professionals. For the range of tenure '1–5 Years', 52.73% of the banking professionals were from Bengaluru and 47.27% from Bhubaneswar, whereas it was 58.7 % and 41.3%, respectively, for IT professionals. For the range of tenure '6–10 Years', about 61.9% of the banking professionals were from Bengaluru and 38.1% from Bhubaneswar, whereas it was equally distributed for the IT professionals. Of the banking professionals who have been serving in the same company for more than 10 years, 57.89% were from Bengaluru and 42.11% from Bhubaneswar, whereas it was equally distributed for the IT professionals.

3.3   Correlation Between Hardiness, the 3Cs, and Role Stress

A researcher uses the basic statistical technique of correlation to determine the degree to which two variables' movements are associated. The correlation technique further helps in determining the presence, direction, and magnitude of the relationship between the independent and dependent variables of the study. We say that two variables are correlated to each other when the value of the correlation coefficient varies from −1 to +1. According to Cohen (1988), an absolute value of r of 0.1 is classified as small, an absolute value of 0.3 is classified as medium, and 0.5 is classified as large. To know the dependency and association between stress and hardiness and its components in our study, I used the correlation technique.

A positive correlation is a relationship between two variables in which both variables move in tandem. A positive correlation exists when one variable decreases as the other variable decreases or one variable increases while the other increases. A negative correlation coefficient exists when an increase in one variable is associated with a decrease in the other variable. In statistics, a perfect positive correlation is represented by 1, while 0 indicates no correlation and −1 indicates a perfect negative correlation.

After Kobasa's initial study on hardiness in 1979, extensive research on stress–hardiness relationship has been done which established the association between both variables as being positive (Kobasa, 1979a; Kobasa, 1982; Kobasa et al., 1982; Kobasa et al., 1982). That is, if the stress of the professionals increases, hardiness also increases. In other terms, when an individual experiences an extreme situation of stressful events, they become hardier in coping with it.

In this study, I have used the Pearson correlation technique to analyse and check whether my findings conform to the earlier studies. Four types of role stresses are normally used to measure stress in professionals. They are SRD, IRD, RB, and PIn. These role stresses were correlated with personality hardiness and its three facets—commitment, control, and challenge. **Table 3.1** represents the correlational relationship between the various components of role stress and hardiness.

From **Table 3.1**, we see that there is a negative correlation between Commitment and SRD, IRD, and PIn (r = −0.082, −0.001, and −0.019,

Table 3.1 Correlation Between Hardiness, the 3cs, and Stress

Dimensions of Hardiness/ Role Stresses		SRD	IRD	RB	PIn
Commitment	Pearson Correlation	−.082	−.001	.156*	−.019
	Sig. (2-tailed)	.212	.983	.017	.777
Control	Pearson Correlation	.155*	.181**	.179**	.165*
	Sig. (2-tailed)	.018	.006	.006	.011
Challenge	Pearson Correlation	−.017	.024	.001	.008
	Sig. (2-tailed)	.802	.720	.987	.904
Tot Hardiness	Pearson Correlation	.001	.007	.203**	.064
	Sig. (2-tailed)	.992	.921	.002	.327
	N	234	234	234	234

Source: Primary data.

*Correlation is significant at the 0.05 level (2-tailed).
**Correlation is significant at the 0.01 level (2-tailed).

respectively). There is a positive and significant correlation between Commitment and RB at the $p < 0.05$ level of significance ($r = 0.156, p = 0.017$). This indicates that hardy professionals who have a strong sense of commitment find it easy to be interested in whatever they are doing and can involve themselves wholeheartedly in a given task. People strong in commitment are rarely at a loss for things to do. They find ways of strategic coping with conflict situations that arise out of RB.

We see a negative correlation between a few role stresses and commitment because the relationship of stress with hardiness and its 3Cs does not always have a unidirectional relationship. As mentioned earlier, hardiness is mostly observed in individuals who are stressed but healthy without having any physical or mental instability. This general level of stress that propels hardiness in an individual might be eustress, or positive stress, which encourages an individual to be motivated and encouraged enough towards better performance and outcomes. Thus, when hardiness increases, stress (in this study, role stresses) decreases. This supports the findings of Vinothkumar et al. (2013) which also showed a negative correlation between perceived stress and the commitment facet of hardiness. Similar findings were obtained from research done by Maddi et al. (2006), in which the three hardy attitudes were significantly but negatively correlated with stress. A negative and significant correlation between hardiness and various role stresses was also obtained in Subramanian and Vinothkumar's study (2009).

The hardiness component—Control—is positively and significantly related with all the dimensions of role stresses—SRD: $r = 0.155, p = 0.018$, where $p < 0.05$; IRD: $r = 0.181, p = 0.006$, where $p < 0.01$; RB: $r = 0.179$, $p = 0.006$, where $p < 0.01$; PIn: $r = 0.165, p = 0.011$, where $p < 0.05$, respectively. The people strong in control believe they can influence the stressful events occurring around them. Qaddumi (2011) explains that people high in control have the ability to develop coping options which are used to see stressful events as part of life (Thomson, 1995), are able to perform and be influential (Orr and Westman, 1990), and a have belief in one's ability to regulate problems (Galla et al., 1994). Hence, events are not taken at the face value but are looked on as how the event could be used to a person's advantage—thus enhancing their coping strategies in dealing with and managing stress. This is in alignment with the findings of Holt et al. (1987), in which the group of elementary teachers who had high levels of stress and burnout earned a higher, although not significantly higher, score for the locus of control scale.

The Challenge component of hardiness has a positive correlation with all the dimensions of role stresses (IRD: $r = 0.024$; RB: $r = 0.001$; PIn: $r = 0.008$) except SRD ($r = -0.017$). However, we do not find any significant relationship between challenge and the dimensions of role stress. The positive association between challenge and the maximum number of role stresses indicates that individuals who possess the challenge component consider it natural to have some amount of stress. They perceive the changes that occur around them as positive and bright opportunities for growth rather than stressful situations. This finding is in contrast to the general belief that life should remain stable as changes in life events cause insecurity and discomfort (Maddi and Kobasa, 1984).

The total hardiness of the professionals is positively correlated with all the four types of role stresses—SRD, IRD, RB, and PIn ($r = 0.001, 0.007, 0.203$, and 0.064, respectively). This supports Kobasa's (1979a) initial research and some other research in succeeding years done by Kobasa and her associates (Kobasa, 1982b; Kobasa et al., 1982) on the stress–hardiness relationship. The general hardiness theory explains that with the increase in stress, there is an increase in the hardiness of the individuals. More important, hardiness acts as a stress-resilience or stress-resistant factor. The protective effects of hardiness in stressful situations are predominantly through cognitive appraisal and coping behaviours. Individuals who are high on hardiness approach life demands actively and perceive that they can handle them successfully. They view them as meaningful and useful, which results in less stressful experiences. Hardy individuals protect themselves by choosing or perceiving the situations that they want to be involved in (Maddi, 1990). These findings are in alignment with Nowack's study (1989), which was based on coping styles in relation to hardiness and health. Results indicated a positive association between stress, coping, and health. Specifically, hardiness was positively correlated with four coping styles. Kobasa et al. (1982) argued that it is important to be hardy if one is experiencing intense stress when they studied the interactive effects of hardiness with stressful life events.

The relationship is meaningful and significant between hardiness and RB at the $p < 0.01$ level of significance because the p-value for the same is 0.002. RB is a conflict a person experiences when they have to choose between living as an individual and as a role occupant. Living as a role occupant, an individual may feel highly stressed out because they feel highly obligated to the expectations of the significant role senders, for which they even sacrifice their own interests, preferences, values, and comforts. This trait is more evident in Indian culture as RB is greater in Indian men and women. A significant relationship between total hardiness and RB shows that hardiness acts as a buffering system or a protective factor in shielding the ill effects of highly stressed and role bounded individuals.

3.4 Descriptive Statistics, ANOVA, and Post Hoc ANOVA— Hardiness and Socio-Demographic Factors Across Sectors and Cities

To represent a sample or even the entire population, researchers use descriptive statistics. Descriptive statistics are generally broken down into measures of central tendency (mean, median, and mode) and measures of variability (standard deviation—*SD* or variance), to summarise the data obtained. Therefore, to understand the features of the sample obtained for this study, I used descriptive statistics like the mean and the standard deviation for all the socio-demographic factors across cities and sectors in relation to hardiness.

The statistical technique of analysis of variance (ANOVA) was used to compare the relationship between two variables across more than two groups. ANOVA helps in examining the means of sub-groups in the sample and analyses the variance as well. Upon further examination, it also helps identify whether the actual values are clustered around the mean or spread out from it. A significant *F*-ratio indicates that the population means are probably not all equal. Wherever required, I used the post hoc ANOVA test also to identify which group mean (or means) has resulted in a significant difference in comparison to the others. This technique precisely helped me in confirming the significance of the effect between the various mean groups.

Table 3.2 depicts the means, the standard deviations, and the significance values of hardiness and its components in relation to gender. The sample descriptive statistics shows that there were 120 male and 114 female

Table 3.2 Descriptive Statistics and ANOVA—Hardiness and Gender

Dimensions of Hardiness	Gender	N	Mean	SD	F	Sig.
Commitment	Male	120	3.5546	.69316	49.373	.000
	Female	114	4.1992	.71009		
	Total	234	3.8686	.77084		
Control	Male	120	2.8773	1.06858	33.499	.000
	Female	114	3.6471	.95971		
	Total	234	3.2523	1.08562		
Challenge	Male	120	3.6417	.82521	.052	.820
	Female	114	3.6667	.85099		
	Total	234	3.6538	.83616		
Tot Hardiness	Male	120	3.5105	.70744	79.900	.000
	Female	114	4.2361	.51377		
	Total	234	3.8640	.71815		

Source: Primary data.

professionals. The sample mean for total hardiness of male professionals is 3.51 and the standard deviation is 0.70, whereas the mean for total hardiness for female professionals is 4.23 and the standard deviation is 0.51. The mean hardiness total score is greater than 3 for both males and females which suggests that the participants of this study were, on average, relatively high on hardiness.

The means for the dimensions Commitment, Control, and Challenge for male professionals are 3.55, 2.87, and 3.64, respectively, whereas the standard deviations are 0.69, 1.06, and 0.82, respectively. The sample means for the female professionals for the dimensions Commitment, Control, and Challenge are 4.19, 3.64, and 3.66, respectively, and the standard deviations are 0.71, 0.95, and 0.85, respectively.

It is evident from the preceding results that the mean is higher for females for all the facets of hardiness in comparison to their male counterparts. This is consistent with Sheard's finding (2009) in which female students reported a significantly higher mean score on hardiness commitment compared to the male students. The mean of overall hardiness for female professionals is also higher in contrast to that of male professionals. This confirms that hardiness is observed more in working women than men in this sample. It might be due to the different coping strategies both hardy men and women employ in stress management. Perceiving or appraising a particular stressor as stressful is also a reason why we find differences in hardiness across gender. For example, a particular stressor might be appraised as stressful for a woman but not for a man. One of the first few studies on the effects of gender on hardiness was done by Barbara Tiller Sanford (1991), who found that high-hardy men had higher self-appraisals and reflected more self-confidence than did high-hardy women, who showed comparatively lower self-appraisals and self-confidence.

Gender variation in hardy coping depends on various coping styles as well. For example, the coping style of men is primarily problem-focused, and for women, it is mostly emotion-focused. Leiter et al. (1994) reported that women used more avoidance or escape types of coping, possibly because they felt powerless to change their work difficulties. Cash and Gardner's study (2011) also support the idea of hardy coping through effective coping strategies as their study show that higher levels of hardiness were associated with more positive appraisals and more effective coping responses.

We also see a significant relationship between gender and hardiness for Commitment and Control as well as for overall hardiness at the $p < 0.01$ level of significance because the p-value is 0.000 for both the dimensions and overall hardiness. However, there is no significant relationship or variance found for challenge in relation to gender. This suggests that gender differences have an effect on hardiness. This significant difference is because of higher means for all the dimensions of hardiness as well as overall hardiness for women compared to their male counterparts.

During the past few decades, women have formed a substantial proportion of the fastest growing segment of the workforce, and they are expected to possess a high degree of career commitment and work involvement. Therefore, women professionals are more likely to view work as another primary role, enhancing a conflict between work and family roles. They need to multitask while having to hold on to their societal norms as well as justify their roles as a professional. They face a lot of stressful situations managing the home front and the workplace at the same time. This is typically found more in Indian culture, where they have to hold onto certain traditional norms which have been created by the society they live in.

Nevertheless, women who are high in commitment and control find meaningful and positive explanations for all the stressful situations life throws at them, and they are equipped enough to influence the things, events, and people around them. Women who are especially high in commitment look at their work at home and at workplace as important and worthwhile enough to warrant their full attention and effort. Women high in control may strategise responses to time and space constraints by making their employment, childcare, and housing decisions in concert (Miranne and Young, 2000). Thus, this hardy coping helps women overcome even extreme role stresses.

Relevant literature so far has sought probable reasons to account for the gender differences in hardiness. As mentioned earlier, one reason might be the differences in the coping strategies both men and women employ (Williams et al., 1992; Klag and Bradley, 2004). Another reason might be the difference between men and women in appraising a particular stressor as stressful (Sanford, 1991; Baum and Grunberg, 1991). Moreover, Klag and Bradley's (2004) research had explained gender differences even when no differences in coping were present. Thus, we can say that hardy female professionals in this sample used more beneficial cognitive and behavioural coping strategies when compared to hardy male professionals when encountering stressful situations.

Yet another study by Holahan and Moos (1985) identified hardiness as a stress-resistance factor which led to the differences in hardy coping among males and females. They identified that stress-resistant men are more self-confident, energetic, and ambitious and that stress-resistant women enjoy qualitatively better social support in the family setting.

Table 3.3 depicts the means, the standard deviations, and the significance values of hardiness and its components in relation to the marital status of corporate professionals. It shows that the sample of this study had 158 married professionals and 76 unmarried professionals. The sample mean of the

Table 3.3 Descriptive Statistics and ANOVA—Hardiness and Marital Status

Dimensions of Hardiness	Marital Status	N	Mean	SD	F	Sig.
Commitment	Married	158	3.9425	.79250	4.539	.034
	Unmarried	76	3.7150	.70412		
	Total	234	3.8686	.77084		
Control	Married	158	3.2686	1.06196	.109	.741
	Unmarried	76	3.2184	1.13971		
	Total	234	3.2523	1.08562		
Challenge	Married	158	3.5886	.86769	2.987	.085
	Unmarried	76	3.7895	.75394		
	Total	234	3.6538	.83616		
Tot Hardiness	Married	158	3.8806	.77656	.260	.611
	Unmarried	76	3.8295	.58143		
	Total	234	3.8640	.71815		

Source: Primary data.

overall hardiness for married professionals is 3.88, with a standard deviation of 0.77, and for unmarried professionals, it is 3.82, with a standard deviation of 0.58.

The sample means for the dimensions Commitment, Control, and Challenge for married professionals are 3.94, 3.26, and 3.58, respectively, and the standard deviations are 0.79, 1.06, and 0.86, respectively. The sample means for the unmarried professionals for the dimensions Commitment, Control, and Challenge are 3.71, 3.21, and 3.78, respectively, and the standard deviations are 0.70, 1.13, and 0.75, respectively. It is evident from the table that the mean is higher for married professionals for the dimensions of Commitment and Control as well as for overall hardiness when compared to the unmarried professionals.

From the ANOVA result, we see that there is a significant relationship between hardiness and marital status for the dimension of Commitment alone at the $p < 0.05$ level of significance because the p-value for the same is 0.034. This is also true because the mean was higher for Commitment for married professionals in comparison to the unmarried professionals. There is no significant relationship or variance found for Control and Challenge and overall hardiness of professionals as far as their marital status is concerned.

Most of the earlier findings of hardiness and its 3Cs in relation to marital status have shown no significant differences (Kobasa, 1979a; Kobasa et al., 1981; Dillard, 1990; Sidhu and Singh, 2016). Another study by D. B. Howard (1996) indicated no significant difference in hardiness on school teachers due to marital status. Similar findings were obtained from Hansen's study (2000) too.

However, my findings suggest the differential effects on hardiness based on the marital status of the professionals. There are very few studies which support my findings. For instance, many years ago, a study by Rhodewalt and Zone (1989) on 212 female college graduates (between ages 25–65) was done to examine the buffering effects of hardiness against stressful life events. The results indicated, particularly for married women, that hardy women are more satisfied with their lives and their husbands than are those who were less hardy. A study by Devi (2014) on the well-being of high school teachers showed that hardiness had an impact on the differences in the well-being of married and unmarried teachers. In other words, married and hardy high school female teachers had a higher sense of wellbeing than unmarried non-hardy teachers.

Table 3.4 depicts the means, the standard deviations, and the significance values of hardiness and its components in relation to age. Out of 234 professionals, the sample of this study had 103 professionals younger than the age of 30, 107 professionals between 30 and 40, and 24 professionals older than 40. The sample means of the overall hardiness for professionals younger than 30, between 30 and 40, and older than 40 are 3.79, 3.86, and 4.17, respectively, and the standard deviations for the three age groups are 0.67, 0.79, and 0.46, respectively.

The sample means for Commitment, Control, and Challenge for professionals younger than 30 are 3.70, 3.11, and 3.62, respectively, and the

Table 3.4 Descriptive Statistics and ANOVA—Hardiness and Age

Dimensions of Hardiness	Age (in years)	N	Mean	SD	F	Sig.
Commitment	Below 30	103	3.7011	.77542	7.345	.001
	30–40	107	3.9274	.77479		
	Above 40	24	4.3258	.47579		
	Total	234	3.8686	.77084		
Control	Below 30	103	3.1169	1.10352		
	30–40	107	3.3314	1.05852	1.626	.199
	Above 40	24	3.4808	1.09977		
	Total	234	3.2523	1.08562		
Challenge	Below 30	103	3.6262	.92722		
	30–40	107	3.6293	.79612	.995	.371
	Above 40	24	3.8819	.53721		
	Total	234	3.6538	.83616		
Tot Hardiness	Below 30	103	3.7947	.67210		
	30–40	107	3.8602	.79079	2.830	.061
	Above 40	24	4.1787	.46296		
	Total	234	3.8640	.71815		

Source: Primary data.

standard deviations for the same group are 0.77, 1.10, and 0.92, respectively. The sample means for Commitment, Control, and Challenge for professionals between 30 and 40 are 3.92, 3.33, and 3.62, and the standard deviations are 0.77, 1.05, and 0.79, respectively. The sample means for Commitment, Control, and Challenge for professionals older than 40 are 4.32, 3.48, and 3.88, and the standard deviations are 0.47, 1.09, and 0.53, respectively.

Thus, it is evident from **Table 3.4** that the mean is highest for all the three dimensions of hardiness as well as the overall hardiness for the professionals 40 years and older. The comparison of the mean scores of three groups of professionals based on their age level reveals that as age increases, the commitment of the professionals to their work and home also increases; they have better control over the things, people and activities around them and can influence them in their favour. They have greater challenging capabilities because of their experience and steadiness.

From the ANOVA results, we see a significant relationship between Commitment and Age at $p < 0.05$, $p = 0.001$. But there is no significant relationship or variance for the dimensions of Control, Challenge, and the overall hardiness as far as the age of professionals is concerned. Therefore, I applied the post hoc ANOVA test to identify which paired mean differences are responsible for this ANOVA result, and it was evident that the mean difference is significant for 'Below 30 Years' and 'Above 40 Years' for both commitment and total hardiness. This significant difference is due to the mean of age group: 40 years and older. Hence, it is confirmed that the aged professionals are hardier and more committed to their work and home. In other words, as age increases, the commitment of professionals to their work and home also increases. A significant variance in age in relation to hardiness and commitment of the professionals suggests that with growing in age, people become more dedicated towards their work and their lives. They find life more interesting and worth living as they grow in age. The experience and maturity of elderly persons enable them to have more stability, meaning, and purpose in life. Thus, age has a significant impact on the level of hardiness, particularly the commitment of professionals in this study.

Our finding agrees with the study of Sandhu et al. (2009), who observed significant differences in the dimensions of commitment of Indian coaches on the basis of their age. Another study by Parkes and Rendall (1988) showed that age accounted for much of the variance in the hardiness scores, especially the different facets of hardiness when the researchers applied multiple regression analysis on the scores of the subjects.

However, a few earlier studies have contradictory findings which did not show any significant difference or relationship between age and hardiness for participants (Kobasa, 1979a; Kobasa et al., 1981; Rhodewalt and Zone, 1989; Benner, 1990; Kelly, 1997; Hansen, 2000).

Table 3.5 depicts the means, the standard deviations, and the significance values of hardiness and the components in relation to the tenure of the professionals. Out of 234 professionals, the sample of this study had 53 professionals who had recently joined the company and had served less than a year, 101 professionals who had served between 1 and 5 years, 43 professionals between 6 and 10 years, and 37 professionals for more than 10 years. The sample means of the overall hardiness for professionals for all the four ranges of tenure are 3.71, 3.86, 3.78, and 4.16, respectively, with standard deviations for the same as 0.88, 0.55, 0.92, and 0.44, respectively.

The professionals who had newly joined and had served less than a year only have sample means for Commitment, Control, and Challenge as 3.78, 3.30, and 3.60, respectively, and standard deviations for the same group is 0.89, 1.25, and 1.03, respectively. The professionals in the range of 1 to 5 years of tenure in the job have sample means for Commitment, Control, and Challenge as 3.77, 3.10, and 3.63, respectively, and standard deviations for the same group are 0.68, 1.04, and 0.81, respectively. The professionals in

Table 3.5 Descriptive Statistics and ANOVA—Hardiness and Tenure

Dimensions of Hardiness	Tenure (in years)	N	Mean	SD	F	Sig.
Commitment	Less than 1	53	3.7870	.89172	4.455	.005
	1–5	101	3.7793	.68080		
	6–10	43	3.8226	.84363		
	More than 10	37	4.2830	.60677		
	Total	234	3.8686	.77084		
Control	Less than 1	53	3.3004	1.25471	1.327	.266
	1–5	101	3.1012	1.04208		
	6–10	43	3.3623	.98756		
	More than 10	37	3.4681	1.03439		
	Total	234	3.2523	1.08562		
Challenge	Less than 1	53	3.6006	1.03844	.237	.870
	1–5	101	3.6337	.81446		
	6–10	43	3.7016	.84949		
	More than 10	37	3.7297	.51871		
	Total	234	3.6538	.83616		
Tot Hardiness	Less than 1	53	3.7168	.88716	3.212	.024
	1 to 5	101	3.8636	.55838		
	6 to 10	43	3.7851	.92893		
	More than 10	37	4.1678	.44053		
	Total	234	3.8640	.71815		

Source: Primary data.

the range of 6 to 10 years in the job have sample means for Commitment, Control, and Challenge as 3.82, 3.36, and 3.70, respectively, and the standard deviations for the same is 0.84, 0.98, and 0.84, respectively. Finally, the professionals who have been working for more than 10 years have sample means for Commitment, Control, and Challenge as 4.28, 3.46, and 3.72, respectively, and standard deviations as 0.60, 1.03, and 0.51, respectively.

It is evident that the mean is highest for the professionals serving more than 10 years in the company for all the three dimensions of hardiness as well as for the overall hardiness. This explains that with the increase in job tenure, professionals become more committed towards their work, have better control over the workplace issues, and are more optimistic and open to challenges and risks in their jobs.

The ANOVA result shows no significant relationship between Control and Challenge of the professionals with Tenure. However, there is a significant relationship between Commitment and the overall hardiness with Tenure at a $p < 0.05$ level of significance because the p-value for commitment is 0.005 and for overall hardiness, 0.024. I applied the post hoc ANOVA test to identify the actual group mean (or means) which shows significant differences when compared to others. The results revealed significant mean differences between the tenure groups of more than 10 years with the other three groups for the dimensions of Hardiness–Commitment. However, for total hardiness, there is only one significant paired comparison between the means of 'More than 10 Years' and 'Less than 1 Year' tenure. It is evident that these significant differences are more so due to the group mean of 'More than 10 Years' than any other group. In other words, the increase in tenure leads to increase in hardiness and commitment level of the professionals towards their organisations. Moreover, when an individual works in the same organisation for a long duration, they develop a strong loyalty and obligation towards it. It is also human to develop an attachment with the work environment, the organisation, and the colleagues they work with. The comfort level of the professionals also increases as they work with known people and known resources around them. Thus, with long tenure, professionals get to know the worth of their work and the positive outcomes it generates.

This finding is also corroborated by Jana Radisic's study (2005), which found that police officers exhibited more hardiness and fewer total stressors as their tenure increased. However, there are also some studies that indicate low or no correlation when hardiness and its sub-components were measured with the subjects' tenure in the current job (Dillard, 1990; Virgin, 1994).

Table 3.6 depicts the means, the standard deviations, and the significance or variance of hardiness and its components in relation to the professionals'

Table 3.6 Descriptive Statistics and ANOVA—Hardiness and LOMs

Dimensions of Hardiness	LOMs	N	Mean	SD	F	Sig.
Commitment	Senior	39	4.3126	.71646		
	Middle	139	3.8230	.77764	9.114	.000
	Junior	56	3.6727	.67909		
	Total	234	3.8686	.77084		
Control	Senior	39	3.5756	1.15413		
	Middle	139	3.1615	1.01971	2.239	.109
	Junior	56	3.2525	1.16989		
	Total	234	3.2523	1.08562		
Challenge	Senior	39	3.7265	.73298		
	Middle	139	3.5731	.83336	1.703	.184
	Junior	56	3.8036	.89731		
	Total	234	3.6538	.83616		
Tot Hardiness	Senior	39	4.1492	.69484		
	Middle	139	3.8786	.63262	6.377	.002
	Junior	56	3.6293	.85603		
	Total	234	3.8640	.71815		

Source: Primary data.

LOM. Out of 234 professionals, the sample of this study had 39 professionals at the senior level, 139 at the middle level, and 56 professionals at the junior level. At the senior level, the sample mean of overall hardiness for professionals is 4.14 with a standard of 0.69; at the middle level, it is 3.87 and 0.63, respectively; and at the junior level, it is 3.62 and 0.85, respectively.

The sample means for the professionals at senior level for Commitment, Control, and Challenge are 4.31, 3.57, and 3.72, respectively, and the standard deviations for the same are 0.71, 1.15, and 0.73, respectively. At the middle level of management, the sample means for the professionals' Commitment, Control, and Challenge are 3.82, 3.16, and 3.57, respectively, and the standard deviations for the same are 0.77, 1.01, and 0.83, respectively. At the junior level, the sample mean for the professionals' Commitment, Control, and Challenge are 3.67, 3.25, and 3.80, respectively, and standard deviations for the same are 0.67, 1.16, and 0.89, respectively.

Except for the dimension of challenge, the mean is highest for Commitment and Control for professionals at the senior level of management. Even the mean for the overall hardiness is highest for the senior-level professionals in comparison to the other two LOMs. This indicates that hardy senior professionals might be internally predisposed to perceive only a few stressors in their environment and can evaluate situations which are less stressful.

The management levels, in any organisation, are distinct categories of responsibilities a professional holds on to. Although the titles and responsibilities may differ from one organisation to another, each level has its specified place within the organisational hierarchy. For senior professionals, especially, the roles and responsibilities are more of policy making and solving major organisational issues. Such major issues, for instance, might be proactively perceiving any threat and turning it into a favourable opportunity for their organisation. They also have the responsibility to manage a large team of professionals working under them.

From the ANOVA results, we find a significant relationship between Overall Hardiness and LOMs at $p < 0.05$, $p = 0.002$. A significant relationship between Commitment and LOMs at $p < 0.01$, $p = 0.000$, is also seen. However, no such variance or significance is found between the other two dimensions of hardiness with respect to the LOMs. Therefore, to get better clarity about which mean group (or groups) is significantly different from the other groups, I applied the post hoc ANOVA test.

The results revealed significant mean differences of the senior level with the other two LOMs for the dimension of Hardiness–Commitment. However, for Hardiness, there is only one significant paired comparison between the means of senior professionals and junior professionals. Therefore, it is evident that these significant mean differences are more so due to the group of senior-level professionals. In other words, we find significant variance in LOMs with Commitment and the total hardiness due to the mean group of senior professionals.

A high-hardy and committed senior professional would give due importance to the values and beliefs of their organisation and its policies. The hardy senior professionals, who are expected to work long hours and solve major organisational issues, are likely to view such work stressors differently than those employees who are low in hardiness do. They might be even influenced by their internal locus of control to perceive situations as less stressful in their surroundings. Moreover, a high sense of commitment is likely to result in professionals being actively engaged in scanning the environment for interesting and stimulating tasks (Eschleman et al., 2010).

However, the findings of Dillard's study (1990) were a bit different with very low correlations and no significance between job level and the subscales of hardiness. Similarly, the first few studies on hardiness also showed no significant difference in hardiness with respect to the level one holds in a job (Kobasa, 1979a; Kobasa et al., 1981).

3.5   Descriptive Statistics, ANOVA, and Post Hoc ANOVA of Stress With Socio-Demographic Factors—Gender, Marital Status, and Age

Interestingly, not all individuals perceive a particular work situation as stressful, nor do those who perceive it as stressful react in the same manner with the same type and degree of outcome (Haw, 1982). Therefore, it is necessary to understand the type and number of stressors that an individual perceives as stressful. This would be of great help to professionals in combatting and coping with a particular stressor (or stressors) in future. Moreover, people face a variety of stressful situations at the same time, generated from different spheres of their lives—especially at home, at work, and in community life. To understand the degree of negative effects of particular role stressors in the work and family life of professionals, I used the descriptive statistical technique. This technique gives a general idea about how the data have been broken down into measures of central tendency and measures of dispersion. With the help of the mean and the standard deviation, one can describe and understand the features of the sample obtained for this study, especially in identifying the group means of various variables. I further used the statistical technique of ANOVA to identify if there is any difference between two or more group means. A significant F-ratio indicates that the population means are probably not all equal.

Table 3.7 shows the means, the standard deviations, and the significance levels of the various role stresses—SRD, IRD, RB, and PIn—of professionals in relation to gender. The sample means for the male professionals for the four role stresses—SRD, IRD, RB, and PIn—are 2.53, 2.20, 2.42, and 2.35, respectively, and the standard deviations for the same are 0.85, 0.89, 0.86, and 1.01, respectively. The sample means for the female professionals for the four role stresses—SRD, IRD, RB, and PIn—are 2.59, 2.20, 3.09, and 2.33, respectively, and the standard deviations for the same are 0.86, 0.95, 0.91, and 0.95, respectively.

Table 3.7 Descriptive Statistics and ANOVA—Stress and Gender

GRS	Gender	N	Mean	SD	F	Sig.
SRD	Male	120	2.5333	.85602	.288	.592
	Female	114	2.5936	.86077		
	Total	234	2.5627	.85702		
IRD	Male	120	2.2028	.89013	.002	.968
	Female	114	2.2076	.95770		
	Total	234	2.2051	.92168		
RB	Male	120	2.4250	.86962	32.377	.000
	Female	114	3.0906	.91988		
	Total	234	2.7493	.95278		
PIn	Male	120	2.3500	1.01239	.023	.879
	Female	114	2.3304	.95369		
	Total	234	2.3405	.98217		

Source: Primary data.

Except PIn, the means are higher for three role stresses, mainly SRD, IRD, and RB, for female professionals than for their male counterparts. In general, working women experience a variety of role stresses than working men in India. In a study done by Nowack (1989) on professional employees attending management training workshops from a variety of organisations in the Los Angeles area, female professionals reported significantly more work and life stress than did male professionals. Yet another study by Dale Alan Snow (1995) showed that women reported higher stressor experiences and higher anxiety than men did. Similar findings were obtained from the study by Cronkite and Moos (1984), in which women were more responsive to stressors than were men.

The ANOVA result shows no significant difference of SRD, IRD, and PIn in relation to gender. However, there is a significant relationship between RB and Gender at the $p < 0.01$ level as the p-value for the same is 0.000. From the descriptive table, it was clear that the means are higher for SRD, IRD, and RB for female professionals than for male professionals. This explains that women are more stressed than their male counterparts and that it is more apparently due to RB than to any other role stresses.

The societal values of being duty-bound towards every additional role that an individual has to perform in the Indian culture contributes to high levels of RB (Eckensberger, 2006). RB is seen more in women in Indian culture because a woman is traditionally regulated by the expectations arising out from various roles that she plays as a daughter-in-law, a mother, and a wife, as well as a working woman. While fulfilling these expectations from the various role senders, they keep sacrificing their own interests, likings, and values. The major reason for role stress among working women in India is also because of the social pressure to conform to the traditional norms inculcated in our culture. The conflict between the normatively prescribed roles for women and those demanded by the modern work environment has resulted in role conflicts of various kinds amongst all working women (Golpelwar, 2016). Women are more affected also by the stress of those around them, as they tend to be more emotionally involved than men in social and family networks (Kessler and McLeod, 1984; Turner et al., 1995).

Although there have been conflicting outcomes in the literature examining the relationship between gender and stress, several authors have determined that women find themselves in stressful circumstances more often than men which support our findings (Almeida and Kessler, 1998; McDonough and Walters, 2001). Another study also found that women experienced more work-related stress in general (Cox et al., 1993). Women are also more likely to report home and family life events as stressful (Oman and King, 2000) and are exposed to more daily stress associated with their routine role functioning (Kessler and McLeod, 1984).

Table 3.8 Descriptive Statistics and ANOVA—Stress and Marital Status

GRS	Marital Status	N	Mean	SD	F	Sig.
SRD	Married	158	2.5907	.90832	.520	.472
	Unmarried	76	2.5044	.74136		
	Total	234	2.5627	.85702		
IRD	Married	158	2.2932	.97118	4.514	.035
	Unmarried	76	2.0219	.78379		
	Total	234	2.2051	.92168		
RB	Married	158	2.8333	.97292	3.831	.052
	Unmarried	76	2.5746	.89044		
	Total	234	2.7493	.95278		
Pin	Married	158	2.3544	1.05522	.098	.754
	Unmarried	76	2.3114	.81529		
	Total	234	2.3405	.98217		

Source: Primary data.

Table 3.8 shows the means, the standard deviations, and the variance between the group means of the various role stresses of the professionals in relation to their marital status. The sample means for the married professionals for the four role stresses—SRD, IRD, RB, and PIn—are 2.59, 2.29, 2.83, and 2.35, respectively, and the standard deviations for the same are 0.90, 0.97, 0.97, and 1.05, respectively. The sample means for the unmarried professionals for the four role stresses—SRD, IRD, RB, and PIn—are 2.50, 2.02, 2.57, and 2.31, respectively, and the standard deviations for the same are 0.74, 0.78, 0.89, and 0.81, respectively.

It is found that the means are higher for the married professionals for all the role stresses compared to that of the unmarried professionals. This means that the occurrence of such role stresses is experienced more in married individuals than in those unmarried. This might be due to the effect of one's distress on the other spouse, resulting in a stressful situation for both partners. A study by Cronkite and Moos (1984) demonstrated that a critical aspect of the stress process among married couples involved the interplay between the functioning, personal coping resources, and coping responses of the partners. They investigated not that only can one spouse's symptoms be a source of stress for the other but that the personal coping resources and coping responses of each partner can also alter the impact of stress and the effectiveness of coping.

From the ANOVA results, we see no significant relationship between SRD, RB, and PIn in relation to marital status. However, there is a significant relationship between IRD and Marital Status at a $p < 0.05$ level of significance because the p-value for the same is 0.035. From the results of the descriptive table, it is evident that the mean is higher for the married professionals for all the role stresses compared to unmarried professionals. This is due to the variety of role occupancies of married couples compared to those unmarried, which determines the range of potentially stressful experiences and thus increases the chance of exposure to some stressors and precludes the presence of others.

IRD is a conflict arising between the organisational and non-organisational roles an individual has to play in their lives. This type of conflict seems more in married individuals as they have to play multiple roles and have multiple responsibilities as well as meet the multiple expectations from the people around them, both at home and at their workplace. For example, an individual has to play the role of a son/daughter-in-law as well as the role of a manager/executive in their job. While juggling the demands and expectations of both roles, they may experience the stress of IRD. After marriage, generally, the role occupancy and responsibilities related to those roles increase, and thereby, the obligations attached to those roles also increase. As Matud (2004) opines, women and men differ in the frequency of their occupancy of social roles and in their experiences within similar social roles. Women's positions at work and in the family are less favourable since they carry a greater burden of demands and limitations (Matthews et al., 1998; Mirowsky and Ross, 1995). Married working women, therefore, experience this type of role stress even more because of the lack of social support from their family and excessive expectations to conform to the socially prescribed roles in India (Golpelwar, 2016).

Table 3.9 depicts the means and the standard deviations of the various role stresses of professionals with respect to their age. The sample means for the professionals younger than 30 for the four role stresses—SRD, IRD, RB, and PIn—are 2.56, 2.10, 2.78, and 2.19, respectively, and the standard deviations for the same are 0.79, 0.83, 0.95, and 0.82, respectively. For the professionals between 30 and 40, the sample means for SRD, IRD, RB, and PIn are 2.60, 2.27, 2.65, and 2.48, respectively, and the standard deviations for the same are 0.89, 0.98, 0.99, and 1.11, respectively. For the professionals who are older than 40, the sample means for SRD, IRD, RB, and PIn are 2.36, 2.34, 3.00, and 2.31, and the standard deviations for the same are 0.95, 0.99, 0.69, and 0.95, respectively.

The means are highest for SRD and PIn for the professionals between 30 and 40, whereas the means for IRD and RB are highest for the professionals who are over 40. This explains the fact that professionals 30 or older are more stressed than those younger than 30. A study done by Bhattacharya and Basu (2007) also says that professionals older than 30 face greater distress/ stress than do those younger than 30. According to the study, as people age, the ability to achieve a relaxation response after a stressful event becomes more difficult. Aging may simply wear out the systems in the brain that respond to stress. Thus, older persons may find it difficult to cope with the great demands of their lives. Moreover, the job sectors nowadays are subject

Table 3.9 Descriptive Statistics and ANOVA—Stress and Age

GRS	Age (in years)	N	Mean	SD	F	Sig.
SRD	Below 30	103	2.5696	.79299		
	30–40	107	2.6012	.89541	.774	.462
	Above 40	24	2.3611	.95258		
	Total	234	2.5627	.85702		
IRD	Below 30	103	2.1036	.83239		
	30–40	107	2.2710	.98322	1.186	.307
	above 40	24	2.3472	.99506		
	Total	234	2.2051	.92168		
RB	Below 30	103	2.7864	.95070		
	30–40	107	2.6573	.99838	1.413	.246
	above 40	24	3.0000	.69505		
	Total	234	2.7493	.95278		
Pin	Below 30	103	2.1974	.82107		
	30–40	107	2.4829	1.11144	2.246	.108
	above 40	24	2.3194	.95036		
	Total	234	2.3405	.98217		

Source: Primary Data.

to continuous and fast-paced changes that require a continuous upgrading of knowledge on the part of the professionals. Learning new skills at a job to keep pace with the fast-growing and competitive technological environment can also cause workplace stress for older individuals.

Although the means are higher for the age groups '30–40' and 'Above 40 Years', I did not find any significant difference between the means of various age groups through the ANOVA. This suggests that age is not the only determining factor which results in different types of roles stresses for this sample; rather, there might be various other factors which influence the stress in those individuals. This supports earlier studies which showed no significant difference between age and stress of the individuals (Kobasa, 1979a; Kobasa et al., 1981; Kelly, 1997). The study by Harilal and Santhosh (2017) has also shown no significant relationship between age and various role stresses like SRD, IRD, RB, and PIn.

3.6 Hardiness and Its 3Cs With Culture

This section explains the relationship of hardiness and its three components (3Cs—each component measured separately) with various facets of Indian culture. I used the statistical technique of ANOVA here again because of the advantage of this statistical technique. The advantage is that it provides the information of main effects as well as the interactive effects of independent variables taken into consideration. As the variables taken in this study are interrelated in real-life situations and develop a multifaceted relation exerting influence on each other, an attempt was made to check the significant variance of hardiness in terms of the cultural background of the professionals.

The multiple regression analysis helps in predicting the value of one variable based on the values of two or more variables, wherein the variable we want to predict is the dependent variable or the outcome variable and the other variables are the independent variables (predictors) whose values decide the impact on the outcome variable. Here, I have used the multiple regression test to predict the impact of Culture (independent variable) on the Overall Hardiness (dependent variable) of these professionals along with the 3Cs (independent variables) of hardiness. Basically, I wanted to assess the significant contribution of Indian culture towards making hardy personalities.

As stated in Chapter 1, this study involves seven aspects of Indian culture: FC, KY, CT, PE, FG, SK, and SR, which have been dealt with in detail in relation to hardiness and its 3Cs (each separately) in the following section.

Table 3.10 explains the relationship of Total Hardiness with seven aspects of culture. From the table, we see a significant relationship and variance between hardiness and a few aspects of culture like PE, FG, and SR at the $p < 0.05$ level of significance as the p-values for PE, FG, and SR are

Table 3.10 ANOVA—Relationship of Total Hardiness With Various Facets of Culture

		Sum of Squares	df	Mean Square	F	Sig.
FC	Between Groups	47.321	43	1.100	1.299	.120
	Within Groups	160.958	190	.847		
	Total	208.279	233			
KY	Between Groups	22.697	43	.528	1.049	.401
	Within Groups	95.591	190	.503		
	Total	118.287	233			
CT	Between Groups	29.277	43	.681	1.179	.226
	Within Groups	109.685	190	.577		
	Total	138.962	233			
PE	Between Groups	72.484	43	1.686	1.528	.029
	Within Groups	209.614	190	1.103		
	Total	282.098	233			
FG	Between Groups	41.086	43	.955	1.519	.031
	Within Groups	119.500	190	.629		
	Total	160.587	233			
SK	Between Groups	23.262	43	.541	.954	.557
	Within Groups	107.692	190	.567		
	Total	130.954	233			
SR	Between Groups	33.830	43	.787	1.447	.049
	Within Groups	103.285	190	.544		
	Total	137.115	233			

Source: Primary data.

0.029, 0.031, and 0.049, respectively. Hardiness does not seem to have any significant effect on other cultural aspects like KY, CT, FC, and SK.

A high-hardy individual is open to the learning experiences that life teaches them and has a control over utilising those experiences which are useful and helpful and which have a meaning or purpose in life. Moreover, hardiness develops through the interaction of the person with others and situations, and as a personality component, it can be increased or decreased by life experiences (Maddi, 1996). This process of learning is ongoing with the growth of the person in life. Such a person finds spirituality through learning and experience and develops greater FG. As Maddi also opines, "the source and direction of spirituality in hardiness is the person's inherent, subjective need to interpret, order, and influence experiences so as to provide meaning in an otherwise indifferent universe" in "[r]elationship of hardiness and Religiousness to depression and anger" (Maddi et al., 2006). Thus, this positive sense of self, purposefulness, self-awareness, spirituality, and knowledge of context and the world also results in socially responsible citizens.

Table 3.11 explains the relationship of Commitment with various aspects of Culture. There is a significant relationship between Commitment and one

Table 3.11 ANOVA—Relationship of Commitment With Various Facets of Culture

		Sum of Squares	df	Mean Square	F	Sig.
FC	Between Groups	26.340	18	1.463	1.729	.036
	Within Groups	181.938	215	.846		
	Total	208.279	233			
KY	Between Groups	7.919	18	.440	.857	.631
	Within Groups	110.368	215	.513		
	Total	118.287	233			
CT	Between Groups	15.117	18	.840	1.458	.108
	Within Groups	123.845	215	.576		
	Total	138.962	233			
PE	Between Groups	23.815	18	1.323	1.101	.352
	Within Groups	258.284	215	1.201		
	Total	282.098	233			
FG	Between Groups	19.387	18	1.077	1.640	.053
	Within Groups	141.200	215	.657		
	Total	160.587	233			
SK	Between Groups	7.684	18	.427	.745	.762
	Within Groups	123.270	215	.573		
	Total	130.954	233			
SR	Between Groups	11.700	18	.650	1.114	.340
	Within Groups	125.416	215	.583		
	Total	137.115	233			

Source: Primary data.

of the parameters of Culture, that is, FC. The significance found is at the $p <$ 0.05 level (p-value is 0.036). However, there is no significance or variation found between Commitment and other cultural aspects like KY, CT, PE, SK, FG, and SR. Commitment in hardiness means having a purpose of life and involvement in family, work, community, society, friends, and religious faith, as well as one's own self. In other words, it gives one meaning to one's life. When one has this commitment to something or someone that is important to us, it gives our life a purpose. Due to this involvement factor, highly committed individuals give utmost importance to their family and inculcate the same cultural values which have been passed on to them from generations to generations. This is the reason why we see highly committed individuals giving more importance to FC—one of the most important aspects of Indian culture. According to N. K. Chadha,

> India, like most other traditional, eastern societies is a collectivist society that emphasizes family integrity, family loyalty, and family unity. More specifically, collectivism is reflected in the readiness to cooperate with family members and extended kin on decisions affecting most aspects of life, including career choice, mate selection, and marriage.
>
> (2012, p. 1)

Dr Radhakrishnan also believes that traditional views still have "a strong hold on Indians" and that "family affections [are] much stronger, than perhaps in any other country" (*Religion and Society*, p. 184).

Table 3.12 explains the relationship of Control with the seven aspects of Culture. There is no significance found between Control and the various aspects of Culture. According to Kobasa, control is the tendency to think, feel, and act as if one is in control of oneself, that one is not helpless but can control the contingencies of life. Individuals in control think that they can make a difference in the world through their exercising imagination, knowledge, skill, and choice. No significance was found between Control and various aspects of Culture, arguably because Indian religious culture does not encourage this trait in an individual. The theory of *karma* or the concept of destiny (*Karmavada*) holds that everything in life and in this world is predetermined and that it is neither possible nor desirable to take control of things and act as God. Besides, the belief in KY reassures an individual to prioritise the performance of duty without any wish for results.

Table 3.13 explains the relationship of Challenge with the various aspects of Indian culture. The p-values for KY, 0.033, and FG, 0.001, with Challenge indicates a significant relationship of challenge, with KY and FG at the $p <$ 0.05 level of significance. These findings suggest that there is a role of the beliefs in KY and FG in accepting and meeting challenges not only

Table 3.12 ANOVA—Relationship of Control With Various Facets of Culture

		Sum of Squares	df	Mean Square	F	Sig.
FC	Between Groups	68.587	70	.980	1.143	.244
	Within Groups	139.692	163	.857		
	Total	208.279	233			
KY	Between Groups	43.593	70	.623	1.359	.058
	Within Groups	74.695	163	.458		
	Total	118.287	233			
CT	Between Groups	42.360	70	.605	1.021	.448
	Within Groups	96.602	163	.593		
	Total	138.962	233			
PE	Between Groups	76.940	70	1.099	.873	.738
	Within Groups	205.158	163	1.259		
	Total	282.098	233			
FG	Between Groups	55.603	70	.794	1.233	.141
	Within Groups	104.984	163	.644		
	Total	160.587	233			
SK	Between Groups	33.702	70	.481	.807	.845
	Within Groups	97.252	163	.597		
	Total	130.954	233			
SR	Between Groups	41.410	70	.592	1.008	.474
	Within Groups	95.705	163	.587		
	Total	137.115	233			

Source: Primary data.

in personal, day-to-day existence but also in the profession of an individual. KY preaches work ethic and arriving at a goal without accepting defeat. As it is bereft of ego, there is no scope of fear of loss. FG imbues in an individual the strength to work against all odds and achieve success.

3.6.1 Regression Analysis: Impact of 3Cs on Hardiness

The following tables show the results of the multiple regression analysis related to the impact of the independent variables—the 3Cs (Challenge, Control, and Commitment) on the dependent variable—Overall Hardiness—of the corporate professionals.

Table 3.14a shows the model summary which provides the R, R-squared, adjusted R-squared, and standard error of the estimate, which determines how well a regression model fits the data obtained. The R (multiple correlation coefficient) value of 0.663 implies a good level of prediction about the impact of the independent variable—the 3Cs on the dependent variable—Hardiness. The R-squared value of 0.440 depicts that our independent

Table 3.13 ANOVA—Relationship of Challenge With Various Facets of Culture

		Sum of Squares	df	Mean Square	F	Sig.
FC	Between Groups	14.403	19	.758	.837	.662
	Within Groups	193.876	214	.906		
	Total	208.279	233			
KY	Between Groups	15.776	19	.830	1.733	.033
	Within Groups	102.512	214	.479		
	Total	118.287	233			
CT	Between Groups	12.394	19	.652	1.103	.349
	Within Groups	126.568	214	.591		
	Total	138.962	233			
PE	Between Groups	21.170	19	1.114	.914	.566
	Within Groups	260.928	214	1.219		
	Total	282.098	233			
FG	Between Groups	29.338	19	1.544	2.518	.001
	Within Groups	131.248	214	.613		
	Total	160.587	233			
SK	Between Groups	16.070	19	.846	1.576	.064
	Within Groups	114.884	214	.537		
	Total	130.954	233			
SR	Between Groups	16.042	19	.844	1.492	.090
	Within Groups	121.074	214	.566		
	Total	137.115	233			

Source: Primary data.

variables (Challenge, Control, and Commitment) explain about 44% of the variability in our dependent variable—Hardiness—and the remaining 56% of the variation is caused by factors other than the predictors included in this model. In addition to this, the adjusted R-squared value of .433 indicates that 43.3% of the variation in the outcome variable is explained by the predictors, which are kept in the model. The standard error of estimate is 0.540. Overall, the results obtained show a very low discrepancy between the values of R-squared and adjusted R-squared, which describes that the model can be considered as a good fit model.

Table 3.14b indicates the statistical significance of the model wherein the F-ratio of the ANOVA tests whether the model is a good fit for the data. As expected, the results obtained here indicate that the 3Cs (independent variables) statistically significantly predict Hardiness (the dependent variable) as $F = 60.293$, where p (.000) $< .05$. Thus, this regression model is a good fit for the data.

Table 3.14c indicates the statistical significance of each of the independent variables, which tests whether the unstandardised (or standardised)

Table 3.14a Determining How Well the Model Fits—Hardiness and Its 3Cs

Model	R	R-Squared	Adjusted R- Squared	Std. Error of the Estimate
1	.663[a]	.440	.433	.54080

a Predictors: (constant), Challenge, Control, Commitment.
b Dependent variable: Hardiness.

Table 3.14b Statistical Significance of the Model—Hardiness and Its 3Cs

ANOVA[a]

Model		Sum of Squares	df	Mean Square	F	Sig.
1	Regression	52.900	3	17.633	60.293	.000[b]
	Residual	67.266	230	.292		
	Total	120.166	233			

a Dependent variable: Hardiness.
b Predictors: (constant), Challenge, Control, Commitment.

Table 3.14c Statistical Significance of the Independent Variables—Hardiness and Its 3Cs

Coefficients

Model	Unstandardised Coefficients		Standardised Coefficients	t	Sig.	Collinearity Statistics	
	B	Std. Error	Beta (β)			Tolerance	Variance Inflation Factor
(Constant)	1.297	.197		6.595	.000		
Commitment	.480	.058	.515	8.279	.000	.628	1.593
Control	.034	.040	.052	.865	.388	.675	1.482
Challenge	.163	.050	.190	3.245	.001	.707	1.414

a Dependent variable: Hardiness.

coefficients are equal to 0 (zero) in the population (i.e. for each of the coefficients). If $p < .05$, the coefficients are statistically significantly different from 0 (zero). The usefulness of these tests of significance is to investigate if each explanatory variable needs to be in the model, given that the others are already there.

Here, in **Table 3.14c**, the *t*-value and corresponding *p*-value are in the "t" and "Sig." columns, respectively, and it depicts that Commitment,

p (.000) < 0.05, and Challenge, p (.001) < 0.05, are significant, but Control is not significant, as p (.388) > 0.05. This means that the explanatory variable Control is no longer useful in the model when the other two variables—Commitment and Challenge—are already in the model. In other words, the dimension of Control no longer adds a substantial contribution in enhancing hardiness in professionals for this sample.

The standard error of the coefficients in the regression output is also intended to be as small as possible. In **Table 3.14c**, except for Control, the standard errors of Commitment (0.058) and Challenge (0.050) are smaller than the corresponding coefficients of (0.480) and (0.163), respectively. The beta column (β) suggests that out of the three components of hardiness, Commitment (0.515) is the highest contributing predictor to explain hardiness in these professionals, the next significant contributor is Challenge (0.190), and last is Control (0.052). This model does not have any multicollinearity effect among the predictors, as the variance inflation factor (VIF) is <10 (or Tolerance >0.1) for all three variables.

3.6.2 Regression Analysis: Impact of Culture—As Another Significant Predictor of Hardiness

The following result tables of the multiple regression analysis are related to the impact of the independent variable—Culture—on the dependent variable—Hardiness—of the corporate professionals. Basically, the thrust is on the significant change that the addition of Culture and its various dimensions bring to the overall 3Cs model of hardiness in corporate professionals.

Table 3.15a shows the model summary, which provides the R, R-squared, adjusted R-squared and the standard error of the estimate, which determines how well a regression model fits the data obtained. The R (multiple correlation coefficient) value of 0.678 implies a good level of prediction about the impact of the independent variable—the 3Cs and various dimensions of Culture—on the dependent variable—Hardiness. The R-squared value of 0.460 depicts that our independent variables (Challenge, Control, Commitment, and various Cultural aspects) explain about 46% of the variability in our dependent variable—Hardiness—and the remaining 54% of the variation is caused by factors other than the predictors included in this model. In addition to this, that the adjusted R-square value of .435 indicates a true variation of 43.5% in the outcome variable as explained by the predictors which are kept in the model. The standard error of estimate is 0.539. Overall, the results obtained show a very low discrepancy between the values of R-squared and adjusted R-squared, which describes that the model can be considered as a good fit model.

Table 3.15b indicates the statistical significance of the model wherein the *F*-ratio of the ANOVA tests indicates whether the model is a good fit for the data. As expected, the results obtained here indicate that the independent variables—the 3Cs, Culture, and its dimensions—statistically significantly predict Hardiness (the dependent variable) as $F = 18.974$, where p (.000) < .05. Thus, this regression model is a good fit for the data.

Table 3.15c indicates the statistical significance of each of the independent variables. The usefulness of these tests of significance is to investigate the significance of each explanatory variable that needs to be in the regression model.

The *t*-values and significance values suggest that only Commitment, p (.000) < 0.05, and Challenge, p (.001) < 0.05, are significant contributors to hardiness for the current sample. The standard errors of Commitment (0.058), Challenge (0.050), PE (0.036), and SK (0.054) are smaller than the corresponding coefficients 0.480, 0.163, .055, and 0.078, respectively. Out of all the components of hardiness and dimensions of Culture, the beta (β) column suggests that Commitment is the highest contributing predictor (0.515) for explaining hardiness in these professionals; the next significant contributor is Challenge (0.190), followed by PE (0.084), SK (0.081), Control (0.63), and CT (−0.050) in comparison to others. This model does not have any multicollinearity effect among the predictors, as the VIF is <10 (or Tolerance >0.1) for all the variables. Thus, we can say that culture and its various aspects do have a significant contribution to hardiness.

Table 3.15a Determining How Well the Model Fits—Inclusion of Culture and Its Dimensions as Predictors to the Existing Model of Hardiness

Model	R	R-Squared	Adjusted R-Squared	Std. Error of the Estimate
1	.678[a]	.460	.435	.53958

a Predictors: (constant), Challenge, Control, Commitment, Culture.
b Dependent variable: Hardiness.

Table 3.15b Statistical Significance of the Model—Hardiness, the 3Cs, and Culture

ANOVA[a]

Model		Sum of Squares	df	Mean Square	F	Sig.
1	Regression	55.241	10	5.524	18.974	.000[b]
	Residual	64.925	223	.291		
	Total	120.166	233			

a Dependent variable: Hardiness.
b Predictors: (constant), SR, Commitment, FC, FG, KY, PE, SK, CT, Challenge, Control.

Table 3.15c Statistical Significance of the Independent Variables—The 3Cs of Hardiness, Culture, and Its Dimensions

Coefficients

Model	Unstandardised Coefficients		Standardised Coefficients	t	Sig.	Collinearity Statistics	
	B	Std. Error	Beta			Tolerance	Variance Inflation Factor
(Constant)	1.161	.333		3.491	.001		
Commitment	.468	.058	.502	8.025	.000	.619	1.615
Control	.042	.040	.063	1.047	.296	.661	1.512
Challenge	.160	.052	.186	3.094	.002	.667	1.499
FC	.009	.042	.011	.204	.839	.805	1.242
KY	.044	.058	.044	.763	.446	.740	1.352
CT	−.047	.054	−.050	−.868	.386	.722	1.384
PE	.055	.036	.084	1.537	.126	.805	1.243
FG	−.040	.046	−.047	−.871	.385	.841	1.189
SK	.078	.054	.081	1.451	.148	.770	1.299
SR	−.044	.053	−.047	−.825	.410	.746	1.340

a Dependent variable: Hardiness.

3.7 ANOVA: Hardiness, Stress, and Culture Across Both Sectors and Cities

The ANOVA test results of the major variables Stress and Hardiness with respect to the two sectors and cities revealed no significant variances between the banking and IT professionals. Similar results were obtained in the test of ANOVA of Culture and its various dimensions in relation to professionals belonging to both the cities. However, when both the sectors are taken into consideration, there is no significant variance between the cultural dimensions and sectors except for KY in the ANOVA results obtained. The KY dimension is significant at $p < 0.05$, $p = 0.035$. It is slightly intriguing why the IT professionals exhibit greater adherence to KY. It may be because IT professionals invariably, being from engineering and technological background, have had a more focused and regimented career education than the other professionals who have had varied backgrounds more open to a comparatively relaxed educational atmosphere.

3.8 Summary of Findings

The **main objective** of this study was to assess role stress and hardiness of Indian corporate professionals and the association between these two variables. From the findings of the correlation tables, we see that the total hardiness of the professionals is positively correlated with all the four types of role stresses—SRD, IRD, RB, and PIn. There is a meaningful and significant relationship between Hardiness and RB at $p < 0.01$, $p = 0.002$. RB is the conflict a person experiences when they have to choose between living as an individual and as a role occupant. Living as a role occupant, an individual may feel highly stressed out because they feel highly obligated to the expectations of the significant role senders, for which they even sacrifice their own interests, preferences, values, and comforts. This is more evident in Indian culture as Indians, both men and women, experience greater RB. A significant relationship between Total Hardiness and RB shows that hardiness acts as a buffering system or a protective factor in shielding the ill effects of highly stressed and role-bounded individuals.

These findings support the literature related to stress–hardiness relationship and confirms that highly stressed individuals are high in hardiness too (Kobasa, 1979a; Kobasa, 1982b; Kobasa et al., 1982; Kobasa et al., 1982). This proves my first hypothesis (Hypothesis 1) and fulfils the first objective of this study.

The **second objective** of this study was to assess the impact of various socio-demographic factors on hardiness in corporate professionals. First, an attempt was made to assess the gender variances in hardiness of these professionals, and an assumption was made that female professionals would be hardier compared to their male counterparts. From the descriptive tables, we saw that the mean Total Hardiness score is greater than 3 for both men and women, which suggests that these professionals are having relatively higher hardiness. The mean is higher for women for all the dimensions of hardiness in comparison with their male counterparts. The mean of overall hardiness for female professionals is also higher in contrast to the male professionals. This is also evident from the ANOVA results, where we see a significant relationship between Gender and Hardiness for Commitment and Control as well as for Total Hardiness at the $p < 0.01$ level of significance because the p-value is 0.000 for both the dimensions and Overall Hardiness. However, there is no significant variance found for Challenge in relation to Gender. This proves **Hypothesis 2a**: that women are hardier than their male counterparts, fulfilling a part of the second objective of this study.

The effect of gender on hardiness has to a great extent been overlooked in the past literature of stress–hardiness relationships, but the preceding findings will support the fact that gender has a varying effect on hardiness. In this study, the variance in gender and the effect being stronger for women than men are consistent with the literature that supports this (Claypoole, 1987; Crowe, 1998; Melissa Gerson, 1998; Bartone and Priest, 2001; Hystad, 2012, Mund, 2017).

Second, an assumption was made to assess the impact of age on hardiness and its components. From the descriptive tables, it is evident that the means are the highest for all the three dimensions of hardiness as well as the overall hardiness for the professionals older than 40. The ANOVA result also shows a significant relationship between Commitment and Age at the $p < 0.05$ level of significance because the p-value is .001. But there is no significant relationship or variance for the dimensions of Control, Challenge, and Total Hardiness as far as the age of the professionals is concerned. The significant relationship between age and commitment suggests that with growing in age, people become more committed towards their work and their lives. They find life to be more interesting and worth living as they grow in age. The experience and maturity of aged persons enable them to have a greater sense of stability, as well as meaning and purpose in life. This finding is consistent with the literature on various subjects of different occupations that supports a positive relationship between age and personality hardiness (Macewen and Barling, 1988; Kenney, 2000; Sandhu et al., 2009; Sheard, 2009; Hannah and Morrissey, 1987). Thus, **Hypothesis 2b**, that older professionals would have greater hardiness than young professionals would, is proved.

Other socio-demographic factors in this study include marital status, tenure, and LOMs. Earlier investigations related to these three factors in relation to hardiness have mostly shown no effects or significance between the variables. However, in this study, the average hardiness of married professionals is higher than that of unmarried professionals, and there is also a significant relationship between marital status and one of the components of hardiness—Commitment—at the $p < 0.05$ level of significance, suggesting the impact of marital status on hardiness and supporting a few studies which had similar findings (Rhodewalt and Zone, 1989; Devi, 2014).

From the descriptive tables, it is evident that the mean is highest for the highly tenured professionals (more than 10 years) for all the three dimensions of hardiness as well as for the overall hardiness. There is also a significant relationship between Commitment and Total Hardiness with Tenure at the $p < 0.05$ level of significance. This explains that with the increase in job tenure, the professionals become more committed towards their work, have better control over the workplace issues, and are more optimistic and open to challenges and risks in their jobs. This supports the study by Jana Radisic (2005). However, there are also a few studies that indicate low or no correlation when hardiness and its sub-components were measured with the subjects' tenure in the current job (Dillard, 1990; Virgin, 1994).

Insofar as the LOMs are concerned, except for the dimension of challenge, the mean was highest for Commitment and Control for professionals at the senior LOM. Even the mean for overall hardiness is highest for the senior-level professionals in comparison to the other two LOMs. There is a significant relationship between Commitment and LOMs at the $p < 0.01$ level of significance and Total Hardiness and LOMs at the $p < 0.05$ level of significance. This explains that the various LOMs and the related responsibilities and obligations have some impact on the hardiness of these professionals. These findings are in contrast to the previous studies which showed low or no correlation and significance when the impact of LOMs was studied on hardiness (Kobasa, 1979a; Kobasa et al., 1981; Dillard, 1990)

The **third objective** of this study was to measure the impact of various socio-demographic factors on the four role stresses experienced by the Indian corporate professionals. It was assumed that female professionals would experience more role stresses than would their male counterparts. I have found that the means were higher for a larger number of stresses like SRD, IRD, and RB (except PIn) for female professionals. There was also a significant relationship between RB and Gender at the $p < 0.01$ level of significance ($p = 0.000$). This supports various other earlier studies which showed the same results (Cronkite and Moos, 1984; Nowack, 1989; Snow, 1995; Almeida and Kessler, 1998; McDonough and Walters, 2001; Cox et al., 1993). The major reason for role stress among working women in India is evidently because of the societal pressure to conform to the traditional norms inculcated in our cultural tradition. The clash between the normatively prescribed roles for women and those demanded by the modern work environment has resulted in role conflicts of various kinds amongst all working women. Thus, these findings fulfil our **Hypothesis 3a** and confirm that working women are more stressed than working men.

Regarding the impact of professionals' marital status on role stresses, it was assumed that the married professionals would experience more stress due to role conflicts than would unmarried professionals. The mean was higher for the married professionals for all the role stresses compared to the unmarried professionals. This suggests that the occurrence of such role stresses is experienced more in married individuals in comparison to unmarried ones. The reason behind such an outcome would be the effect of one's distress (related to an adverse and negative event) about the other spouse, which, in turn, results in a stressful situation for both partners (Cronkite and Moos, 1984). The investigation by Cronkite and Moos (1984) found that not only can one spouse's symptoms be a source of stress for the other, but the personal coping resources and coping responses of each partner can alter the impact of stress and the effectiveness of coping. From the test of variance, it was clear that there was a significant relationship between IRD and marital status at $p < 0.05$, $p = 0.035$. After marriage, generally the roles, occupancy, and roles related responsibilities also increase, and thereby, the obligations attached to those roles also increase; therefore, married individuals have more stress induced by IRD. This fulfils **Hypothesis 3b** and hence, that there lies a difference in experiencing the kinds and number of role stresses in relation to the marital status of the professionals is accepted.

Although the means were highest for SRD and PIn for the professionals aged between 30 and 40 and the means for IRD and RB were highest for the professionals who were older than 40 years, no significant difference was found between the means of various age groups through the ANOVA. This suggests that age is not the only determining factor which results in different types of roles stresses; there might be various other factors which influence the stress in these individuals. These findings support a few earlier studies which also showed no significant difference between the age and stress of the individuals (Kobasa, 1979a; Kobasa et al., 1981; Kelly, 1997). The study by Harilal and Santhosh (2017), in particular, shows no significance between age and various role stresses, such as SRD, IRD, RB, and PIn. Thus, I reject **Hypothesis 3c** as I did not find any difference between the stress of the professionals based on their age in this sample.

The **fourth objective** of this study was to assess the relationship between hardiness and its 3Cs with various aspects of culture and that culture can also contribute to making hardy professionals. I used the ANOVA to test the significance between these two variables and their components/dimensions.

When I measured the total hardiness score with various aspects of culture, I found significant relationship and variance between hardiness and a few aspects of culture, such as PE, FG, and SR at the $p < 0.05$ level of significance as the p-values for PE, FG, and SR were 0.029, 0.031, and 0.049, respectively. A high-hardy individual is always open to the learning experiences that life teaches them and has control over utilising those experiences which are useful and helpful and has a purpose in life. This process of learning becomes ongoing as and when the person grows in life. Such a person finds spirituality through learning and experience and develops more FG. In 'Relationship of Hardiness and Religiousness to Depression and Anger', Maddi et al. (2006) also opine that "the source and direction of spirituality in hardiness is the person's inherent, subjective need to interpret, order, and influence experiences so as to provide meaning in an otherwise indifferent universe" (p. 148). Thus, this positive sense of self, purposefulness, self-awareness, experiences, spirituality, and knowledge of context and the world results in socially responsible citizens too.

When I measured commitment, a facet of hardiness, with the various cultural aspects, I found that it was related significantly with one of the parameters of Culture, that is, FC. The significance found was at the $p < 0.05$ level (where the p-value is 0.036). Commitment in hardiness means having a purpose of life and involvement in family, work, community, social, friends, religious faith, our own selves, and the like, that is giving us meaning to our lives. When we have this commitment to something or someone that is important to us, this gives our life a purpose. Owing to this involvement factor, highly committed individuals give the utmost importance to their family and inculcate the same cultural values which have been passed on from generation to generation. This is the reason why we see individuals with high commitment giving more importance to FC—one of the most important aspects of Indian culture.

I did not find any relationship of control (a facet of hardiness) with the various cultural dimensions, but a test of significance of challenge with the dimensions of Culture showed a significant relationship with KY and FG at the $p < 0.05$ level of significance ($p = 0.033$ and 0.001, respectively). This suggests that there is a role for the beliefs in KY and FG in accepting and meeting challenges not only in personal, day-to-day existence but also in the professional life of an individual. KY preaches work ethic and arriving at a goal without accepting defeat. As it is bereft of ego, there is no scope of fear of loss. FG imbues an individual with the strength to work against all odds and achieve success.

Findings from the multiple regression analysis suggest a significant change in the value of R from a value of 0.663 to 0.678 when culture and its dimensions were introduced in the model. This implies a good level of pre-diction about the positive impact of the independent variable—Culture— and its various dimensions on the dependent variable—Hardiness. There was also an increase in the R-squared value from 0.440 to 0.460 which suggests that the inclusion of Culture and its dimensions as independent variables explained more variation and impact on Hardiness than before. Furthermore, the variation in the outcome variable—Hardiness—due to its predictors was more evident when the adjusted R-squared value of 0.433changed to 0.435 after the addition of Culture. The standard error of estimate came down from 0.540 to 0.539.

When Culture was included, the ANOVA results also depicted a signifi-cant F-value, $18.974, p$ ($.000$) $< .05$. The beta values in the coefficients table suggested that Commitment was the highest contributing (0.515) predic-tor for explaining hardiness in these professionals, followed by Challenge (0.190), then PE (0.084), SK (0.081), Control (0.63) and CT (-0.050) in comparison to others. There was no multicollinearity effect among the pre-dictors. Hence, the inclusion of Culture as another significant contributor of Hardiness to the existing model of 3Cs can be considered as a good fit model.

From the preceding findings, we can say that culture does contribute towards making hardy individuals, thus accepting **Hypothesis 4** and fulfill-ing the fourth objective of my study.

The **fifth and the last objective** of this study was to assess the signifi-cant differences between the IT and banking professionals in Bengaluru and Bhubaneswar cities with respect to the levels of role stress, hardiness, and different aspects of Indian culture. The results obtained from the ANOVA tests revealed no significant variances in the various role stresses experienced by the IT and banking professionals living in Bhubaneswar and Bengaluru cities. There was no significant difference in the overall hardiness of these professionals with respect to the different cities and sectors they belong to. I found KY to be one of the important determinants of culture in IT professionals rather than banking professionals. However, there was no major variation found in this sample when I tried to measure cultural variations in both cities, mainly because Indian culture is a unified system. Hence, **Hypothesis 5** is partially accepted.

References

Adnal, M. Bhubaneswar, the only Indian city among World's top global smart city ranking. Updated: Thursday, March 15, 2018, 9:45 [IST]. www.oneindia.com/india/bhubaneswar-the-only-indian-city-among-worlds-global-smart-city-ranking-2658436.html

Almeida, D. M., and Kessler, R. C. (1998). Everyday stressors and gender differences in daily distress. *Journal of Personality and Social Psychology, 75*, 670–680.

Bartone, P. T., and Priest, R. F. (2001). Sex differences in hardiness and health among West point cadets. Paper Presented at the 13th Annual Convention of the American Psychological Society, Toronto. www.hardiness-resilience.com

Baum, A., and Grunberg, N. E. (1991). Gender, stress, and health. *Health Psychology, 10*, 80–85. http://dx.doi.org/10.1037/0278-6133.10.2.80

Benner, C. V. (1990). The relationships of spiritual well-being, selected demographic variables, spiritual variables, health indicators, and AIDS related activities to hardiness in persons who were HIV+ or were diagnosed with ARC or AIDS. Dissertation, University of Maryland College Park. UMI, Ann Arbor, USA. Retrieved from ProQuest Digital Dissertations.

Bhattacharya, S., and Basu, J. (2007). Distress, wellness and organizational role stress among IT professionals: Role of life events and coping resources. *Journal of the Indian Academy of Applied Psychology, 33*(2), 169–178.

Cash, M. L., and Gardner, D. (2011). Cognitive hardiness, appraisal and coping: Comparing two transactional models. *Journal of Managerial Psychology, 26*(8), 646–664. http://dx.doi.org/10.1108/02683941111181752

Chadha, N. K. (2012). Intergenerational relationships: An Indian perspective. www.un.org/esa/socdev/family/docs/egm12/CHADHA-PAPER.pdf

Claypoole, K. H. J. (1987). The impact of stressful life events on illness rates and immune functioning as moderated by type A behaviour, hardiness, loneliness, nutrition and exercise. Dissertation. University of Wyoming. UMI, Ann Arbor, USA. Retrieved from ProQuest Digital Dissertations.

Cohen, J. (1988). *Statistical power analysis for the behavioral sciences* (2nd ed.). Hillsdale, NJ: Erlbaum.

Cox, T., Kuk, G., and Leiter, M. P. (1993). Burnout, health, work stress, and organizational healthiness. In W. B. Schaufeli, C. Maslach, and T. Marek (Eds.), *Series in applied psychology: Social issues and questions: Professional burnout: Recent developments in theory and research* (pp. 177–193). Philadelphia: Taylor & Francis.

Cronkite, R. C., and Moos, R. H. (1984). The role of predisposing and moderating factors in the stress-illness relationship. *Journal of Health and Social Behaviour*, *25*(4), 372–393.

Crowe, L. A. S. (1998). Hardiness, one of several personality constructs thought to affect health. Dissertation, Division of Research and Advanced Studies of the University of Cincinnati. UMI, Ann Arbor, USA. Retrieved from ProQuest Digital Dissertations.

Devi, M. (2014). Well-being of high school female teachers in relation to their marital status and personality hardiness. *Online International Interdisciplinary Research Journal*, *4*(4), 185–192.

Dillard, N. L. (1990). Hardiness and academic achievement. Dissertation, Indiana University School of Nursing. UMI, Ann Arbor, USA. Retrieved from ProQuest Digital Dissertations.

Eckensberger, L. H. (2006). The mutual relevance of indigenous psychology and morality. In U. Kim, K.-S. Yang, and K.-K. Hwang (Eds.), *Indigenous and cultural psychology: Understanding people in context* (pp. 225–245). New York: Springer. http://indigenouspsych.org/Resources/Indigenous%20and%20Cultural%20Psychology%20-%20Understanding%20People%20in%20Context.pdf

Eschleman, K. J., Bowling, N. A., and Alarcon, G. (2010). A meta-analytic examination of hardiness. *International Journal of Stress Management*, *17*(4), 277–307.

Galla, J. P., Hyman, D. M., Stewart, C. T., and Fehr, L. A. (1994). The relationship between cognitive and psychological response to stress. National Social Science Association Conference, Lass Vegas, NV.

Gerson, M. (1998). The relationship between hardiness, coping skills, and stress in graduate students. Dissertation, Adler School of Professional Psychology. UMI, Ann Arbor, USA. Retrieved from ProQuest Digital Dissertations.

Golpelwar, M. K. (2016). *Global call center employees in India: Work and life between globalization and tradition*. Internationale Wirtschafts Partner, Springer Fachmedien Wiesbaden. DOI: 10.1007/978-3-658-11867-9_2

Hannah, T. E., and Morrissey, C. (1987). Correlates of psychological hardiness in Canadian adolescents. *The Journal of Social Psychology*, *127*(4), 339–344.

Hansen, C. (2000). Is there a relationship between hardiness and burnout in full-time staff nurses versus per diem nurses? Dissertation, Grand Valley State University. UMI, Ann Arbor, USA. Retrieved from ProQuest Digital Dissertations.

Harilal, A., and Santhosh, V. A. (2017). A comparative study on stress levels among working women and housewives with reference to the state of Kerala. *NMIMS Journal of Economics and Public Policy*, *2*(1), 29–35.

Haw, M. A. (1982). Women, work, and stress: A review and agenda for the future. *Journal of Health and Social Behaviour*, *23*(2), 132–144.

Holahan, C. J., and Moos, R. H. (1985). Life stress and health: Personality, coping, and family support in stress resistance. *Journal of Personality and Social Psychology*, *49*(3), 739–747.

Holt, P., Fine, M. J., and Tollefson, N. (1987). Mediating stress: Survival of the hardy. *Psychology in the Schools*, *24*, 51–58.

Howard, D. B. (1996). The effect of hardiness efficacy and related educator characteristics on health, stress and burnout. Retrieved from ProQuest Digital Dissertations. (DAI-A 57/09).

Hystad, S. W. (2012). Exploring gender equivalence and bias in a measure of
psychological hardiness. *International Journal of Psychological Studies, 4*(4),
69–79.

Kelly, M. B. (1997). The effect of work-related and personal demographic variables
on burnout and hardiness in nurse managers. Thesis proposal presented to the
Faculty of the Department of Nursing, Clarkson College. UMI, Ann Arbor, USA.
Retrieved from ProQuest Digital Dissertations.

Kenney, J. W. (2000). Women's "inner-balance": A comparison of stressors, personality traits and health problems by age groups. *Journal of Advance Nursing,
31*(3), 639–650.

Kessler, R. C., and McLeod, J. D. (1984). Sex differences in vulnerability to undesirable life events. *American Sociological Review, 49,* 620–631.

Klag, S., and Bradley, G. (2004). The role of hardiness in stress and illness: An
exploration of the effect of negative affectivity and gender. *British Journal of
Health Psychology, 9,* 137–161.

Kobasa, S. C. (1979a). Stressful life events, personality, and health: An inquiry into
hardiness. *Journal of Personality and Social Psychology, 37,* 1–11.

Kobasa, S. C. (1982b). The hardy personality: Toward a social psychology of stress
and health. In G. Sanders and J. Suls (Eds.), *Social psychology of health and illness* (pp. 3–32). Hillsdale, NJ: Erlbaum.

Kobasa, S. C., Maddi, S. R., and Courington, S. (1981). Personality and constitution as mediators in the stress-illness relationship. *Journal of Health and Social
Behaviour, 22*(4), 368–378.

Kobasa, S. C., Maddi, S. R., and Kahn, S. (1982). Hardiness and health: A prospective study. *Journal of Personality and Social Psychology, 42,* 168–177. http://
dx.doi.org/10.1037/0022-3514.42.1.168

Kobasa, S. C., Maddi, S. R., and Puccetti, M. C. (1982). Personality and exercise
as buffers in the stress-illness relationship. *Journal of Behavioral Medicine, 5,*
391–404.

Leiter, M. P., Clark, D., and Dump, J. (1994). Distinct models of burnout and commitment among men and women in the military. *Journal of Applied Behavioral
Science, 30*(1), 63–82.

Macewen, K. E., and Barling, J. (1988). Interrole conflict, family support and marital adjustment of employed mothers: A short term, longitudinal study. *Journal of
Organizational Behaviour, 9,* 241–250.

Maddi, S. R. (1990). Issues and interventions in stress mastery. In H. S. Friedman
(Ed.), *Personality and Disease* (pp. 121–154). New York: Wiley.

Maddi, S. R. (1996). *Personality theories: A comparative analysis* (6th ed.). Pros-
pect Heights, IL: Waveland Press.

Maddi, S. R., Brow, M., Khoshaba, D. M., and Vaitkus, M. (2006). Relationship of
hardiness and religiousness to depression and anger. *Consulting Psychology Journal: Practice and Research, 58*(3), 148–161. DOI: 10.1037/1065-9293.58.3.148

Maddi, S. R., Harvey, R. H., Khoshaba, D. M., Lu, J. L., Persico, M., & Brow, M. (2006). The Personality Construct of Hardiness, III: Relationships with repression, innovativeness, authoritarianism, and performance. *Journal of Personality, 74* (2), 575–598.

Maddi, S. R., and Kobasa, S. C. (1984). *The hardy executive: Health under stress.* Homewood, IL: Dow Jones-Irwin.

Matthews, S., Hertzman, C., Ostry, A., and Power, C. (1998). Gender, work roles and psychosocial work characteristics as determinants of health. *Social Science and Medicine, 46,* 1417–1424.

Matud, M. P. (2004). Gender differences in stress and coping styles. *Personality and Individual Differences, 37,* 1401–1415.

McDonough, P., and Walters, W. (2001). Gender and health: Reassessing patterns and explanations. *Social Science & Medicine, 52,* 547–559.

Miranne, K. B., and Young, A. H. (Eds.) (2000). *Gendering the city: Women, boundaries and visions of urban life.* Oxford, England: Rowman and Littlefield Publishers, Inc.

Mirowsky, J., and Ross, C. E. (1995). Sex differences in distress: Real or artefact? *American Sociological Review, 60,* 449–468.

Mund, P. (April 2017). Are women hardier? A study on Indian corporate professionals. *Paripex: Indian Journal of Research, 6*(4), 530–531. www.worldwidejournals.com/paripex/article/are-women-hardier-a-study-on-indian-corporate-professionals/NzA1Mg==/?is=1

Nowack, K. M. (1989). Coping style, cognitive hardiness, and health status. *Journal of Behavioral Medicine, 12*(2), 145–158.

Oman, R. F., and King, A. C. (2000). The effect of life events and exercise program format on the adoption and maintenance of exercise behaviour. *Health Psychology,* 605–612.

Orr, E., and Westman, M. (1990). Does hardiness moderate stress and how? Learned resourcefulness: On coping skills, self control, and adaptive behaviour. In M. Rosenbaum (Ed.), *Springer series on behavior therapy and behavioral medicine, Vol. 24. Learned resourcefulness: On coping skills, self-control, and adaptive behavior* (pp. 64–94). New York: Springer Publishing Co.

Pareek, U. (2002). *Training instruments in HRD and OD* (2nd ed.), New Delhi: Tata McGraw Hill Publishing Company Ltd.

Parkes, K. R., and Rendall, D. (1988). The hardy personality and its relationship to extraversion and neuroticism. *Journal of Personality and Individual Differences, 9*(4), 785–790.

Qaddumi, H. (2011). The influence of selected demographic variableson hardiness of EFL teachers in palestine. *Journal of Al-Quds Open University for Research and Studies, 25*(1), 13.

Radhakrishnan, S. (1947). *Religion and society.* London: George Allen & Unwin Ltd.

Radisic, J. (2005). Police hardiness and officer's length of service. Dissertation, Chicago School of Professional Psychology. UMI, Ann Arbor, USA. Retrieved from ProQuest Digital Dissertations.

Rhodewalt, F., and Zone, J. B. (1989). Appraisal of life change, depression and illness in hardy and non-hardy women. *Journal of Personality and Social Psychology, 56*(1), 81–86.

Sandhu, K. S., Sharma, R. K., and Singh, A. (2009). Personality hardiness of Indian coaches in relation to their age and coaching experience. *Journal of Exercise Science and Physiotherapy*, *5*(1), 38–41.

Sanford, B. T. (1991). The effects of hardiness and gender on psychophysiological reactivity to two types of stressors. Dissertation, Texas A & M University. UMI, Ann Arbor, USA. Retrieved from ProQuest Digital Dissertations.

Sheard, M. (2009). Hardiness commitment, gender, and age differentiate university academic performance. *British Journal of Educational Psychology*, *79*, 189–204.

Sidhu, R., and Singh, B. (2016). Study of personality hardiness in relation to gender, locality, organisational set-up and marital status. *ZENITH International Journal of Multidisciplinary Research*, *6*(1), 110–115. zenithresearch.org.in

Snow, D. A. (1995). Personality correlates of adolescent stress coping responses. Dissertation, Michigan State University. UMI, Ann Arbor, USA. Retrieved from ProQuest Digital Dissertations.

Subramanian, S., & Vinothkumar, M. (2009). Hardiness Personality, Self-Esteem and Occupational Stress among IT Professionals, *Journal of the Indian Academy of Applied Psychology*, 35, Special Issue, 48–56.

Thomson, W. C. (1995). The contribution of school climate and hardiness to the level of alienation experienced by student teachers. *Journal of Education*, *88*(5), 269–274.

Turner, R. J., Wheaton, B., and Lloyd, D. A. (1995). The epidemiology of social stress. *American Sociological Review*, *60*, 194–205.

Vinothkumar, M., Vinu, V., and Anshya, R. (2013). Mindfulness, hardiness, perceived stress among engineering and BDS students. *Indian Journal of Positive Psychology*, *4*(4), 514–517.

Virgin, S. E. M. (1994). Perceived stress and hardiness in female deans of schools of nursing. Dissertation, University of Alabama at Birmingham. UMI, Ann Arbor, USA. Retrieved from ProQuest Digital Dissertations.

Williams, P. G., Wiebe, D. J., and Smith, T. W. (1992). Coping processes as mediators of the relationship between hardiness and health. *Journal of Behavioral Medicine*, *15*, 237–255. http://dx.doi.org/10.1007/BF00845354

4 Findings and Conclusion

4.1 Prelude to the Study

The adverse effect of work stress on professionals has been studied on a variety of subjects like managers (Kobasa, 1979a, 1981; Kobasa et al., 1982; Kobasa et al., 1982), bus drivers (Bartone, 1984), military men and women (Bartone et al., 1989; Leiter et al., 1994; Bartone, 1995; Bartone, 2007; Bartone, 2013), politicians and ministers (Payne, 1990), police officers (Radisic, 2005; Bano, 2013), geriatric nurses (Duquette et al., 1995), clinical psychologists and counsellors (Cushway and Tyler, 1994; Sowa et al., 1994), and men and women in management positions (Beena and Poduval, 1992; Decker and Borgen, 1993; van der Pompe and de Heus, 1993). However, there has hardly been any study on the work-related stress in Indian corporate professionals. The last three decades have seen major changes in the corporate world due to liberalisation, globalisation, and the information technology (IT) revolution. There has been an intense struggle in various banks and IT companies to excel against others in the present-day cut-throat, competitive world, especially after globalisation and liberal economy.

In this ongoing process of 'survival of the fittest', the professionals in these two sectors have been working under unprecedented pressure and have been experiencing extremely stressful situations. Moreover, doing a target-oriented job and meeting deadlines of IT projects or monthly/quarterly targets in banks have added to the stress levels in these professionals on a daily basis. These work–life hassles and role stresses can lead to negative physical and psychological consequences. An individual also experiences role stresses that stem from various organisational and non-organisational demands in their surroundings and these demands need to be managed properly to control stress in the professionals.

Keeping in view the previously discussed stress-related problems, the present research was undertaken to study the efficacy of hardiness, a personality disposition, in Indian corporate professionals who face stressful situations both in organisational and non-organisational contexts. In this study, I made an attempt to identify the positive/functional stress (eustress) which triggers hardiness in the professionals, which also means that stress is not always perilous to individuals. Sometimes, mild stress can also stimulate the performance of an individual. Since there are individual differences in adaptation and coping, what is 'mild' stress to one may be 'major' stress to another.

Stress has individual, organisational, social and environmental dimensions. One of the major areas of research appears to be organisational stress, in general, and stresses, in particular. Therefore, in this study, I have included four major types of role stresses developed by Udai Pareek (2002) to measure the job-related stress of the corporate professionals.

To study the efficacy of hardiness in reducing the adverse effects of stress, I used a modified version of Bartone's DRS-15 (1995). This tool was helpful in measuring hardiness and its three components of the corporate professionals.

Although many earlier studies have indicated the effect of one's culture on personality vis-à-vis occupational stress and coping strategies, the role of Indian culture in shaping an individual's personality, hardy or otherwise, has not been sufficiently or convincingly studied. So I made an attempt to identify a meaningful relationship between hardiness and a few cultural aspects of India.

The sample of this study was drawn from a population of corporate professionals working in banks and IT companies in two cities in India. The sample obtained consisted of 234 respondents, of which 123 were from Bengaluru and 111 from Bhubaneswar. There were 120 respondents from the banking sector and 114 from the IT sector. The sample included 51% male and 49% female respondents, having nearly 44% of professionals younger than 30, about 46% professionals between 30 and 40, and the remaining 10% older than 40. The percentage of married professionals (68%) was higher than unmarried professionals (32%) and constituted about 23% professionals who have served a tenure of less than 1 year, 43% between 1 and 5 years, 18% between 6 and 10 years, and 16% having a tenure of more than 10 years. Based on the LOMs/seniority, middle-level professionals (59%) constituted the highest percentage of the sample, compared to those in junior-level (24%) and senior-level (17%) management.

The analysis of the results was based on the data collected from the primary source keeping in view the objectives of my investigation. The primary data for this study were collected through the psychometric instruments and data sheet for socio-demographic factors from the corporate professionals mainly working in banks and IT companies and belonging to two cities, Bengaluru and Bhubaneswar. This information sheet/composite questionnaire was emailed to the professionals. The data were collected from two different cities in order to identify the variation (if any) in results with respect to role stress, hardiness, and culture.

The raw data collected from the primary source were analysed with the help of statistical techniques like descriptive statistics, correlation, analysis of variance (ANOVA), post hoc ANOVA and Multiple Regression analysis with the help of the software: SPSS, Version 16.0.

The major findings related to the objectives of this study are summarised next.

4.2 Major Findings

- The overall hardiness of the professionals was positively correlated with all the four types of role stresses—SRD, IRD, RB, and PIn. There was a meaningful and significant relationship between Hardiness and RB at the $p < 0.01$ level of significance, $p = 0.002$. These findings support the literature related to stress–hardiness relationship which reveals that highly stressed individuals are high in hardiness too (Kobasa, 1979a, 1982b; Kobasa et al., 1982; Kobasa et al., 1982). Hence, **Hypothesis 1** is proved, and this also fulfils the first objective of this study.
- There was a significant relationship between Gender and Hardiness for Commitment and Control as well as for Total Hardiness at the $p < 0.01$ level of significance, $p = 0.000$ for both the dimensions and overall hardiness. However, there was no significant variance found for Challenge in relation to Gender. The female professionals were found to be hardier than their male counterparts. The effect of gender on hardiness has been quite overlooked in the past literature of stress–hardiness relationships, but the preceding findings establish the fact that gender has a varying effect on hardiness. The outcome of my study related to hardiness and gender is consistent with the earlier findings by various researchers who also found that women have stronger effects of hardiness than do men (Claypoole, 1987; Crowe, 1998; Melissa Gerson, 1998; Bartone and Priest, 2001; Hystad, 2012). Hence, my **Hypothesis 2a** that women professionals are hardier than the male professionals in this sample, is proved to be true.
- When I tried to find out the relationship between the age of the professionals and the hardiness of those professionals, there was a significant relationship between Commitment and Age at $p < 0.05$, $p = 0.001$. However, I did not find any significance or variance for the dimensions of Control, Challenge, and Total Hardiness insofar as the age of the professionals is concerned. When I applied the post hoc ANOVA test,

I found that the significant difference is due to the mean of age group: 'Above 40 years'. It is, therefore, confirmed that older professionals are hardier and more committed to their work and home than their younger counterparts are. In other words, as age increases, the commitment of professionals to their work and home also increases. These findings also comply with a few other studies wherein age accounted for much of the variance in the hardiness scores, especially the different facets of hardiness (Parkes and Rendall, 1988; Sandhu et al., 2009). These findings also show consistency with earlier studies on various subjects of different occupations that support a positive relationship between age and personality hardiness (Macewen and Barling, 1988; Kenney, 2000; Sheard, 2009; Hannah and Morrissey, 1987). Thus, **Hypothesis 2b,** that older professionals are hardier than younger professionals, is accepted, thereby fulfilling the second objective of this study.

- The assumption that female professionals would experience more role stresses than their male counterparts was also found to be true, thereby proving **Hypothesis 3a**. The mean was higher for a larger number of stressors like SRD, IRD, and RB (except PIn) for female professionals than for male professionals. There was also a significant relationship between RB and Gender at the $p < 0.01$ level of significance ($p = 0.000$). Similar findings were seen in other earlier studies which showed the variation in gender in experiencing different role stresses (Cronkite and Moos, 1984; Nowack, 1989; Cox et al., 1993; Snow, 1995; Almeida and Kessler, 1998; McDonough and Walters, 2001).

  Insofar as the marital status of the individuals was concerned, the assumption that married professionals experience a variety of roles stressors compared to unmarried professionals was also found to be true. The means were higher for the married professionals for all the role stresses compared to unmarried professionals. From the ANOVA, it was clear that there was a significant relationship between IRD and Marital Status at $p < 0.05$, $p = 0.035$. Hence, this fulfilled **Hypothesis 3b**.

- There was no significance between the professionals' age and various role stresses like SRD, IRD, RB, and PIn, so **Hypothesis 3c** could not be accepted. This suggests that age is not the only determining factor which results in different types of roles stresses; rather, there might be various other factors which influence the stress in these individuals. These findings support a few earlier studies which also show no significant difference between age and stress of the individuals (Kobasa, 1979a; Kobasa et al., 1981; Kelly, 1997). The study by Harilal and Santhosh (2017) also did not show any significance between age and various role stresses like SRD, IRD, RB, and PIn.

- The **fourth objective** of this study was to assess the relationship between hardiness and its 3Cs with various aspects of Indian culture. ANOVA was used to assess the significance between these two variables and their various components/dimensions. When I measured the total hardiness score with the various aspects of culture, I found significant relationship and variance between hardiness and a few aspects of culture like PE, FG, and SR at $p < 0.05$, where $p = 0.029, 0.031$, and 0.049, respectively.

Furthermore, when I measured Commitment, a facet of hardiness, with the various cultural aspects, I found that it was related significantly with only one parameter of culture, that is, FC at the $p < 0.05$ level (where $p = 0.036$). However, I did not find any significant relationship between control and various cultural dimensions. Nevertheless, a significant relationship was found between challenge and the two dimensions of culture: KY and FG at $p < 0.05$, $p = 0.033$ and 0.001, respectively.

The regression analysis showed a significant change in the value of R from a value of 0.663 to 0.678 when Culture and its dimensions were introduced in the existing model. This implies a positive impact of the independent variable—Culture—and its various dimensions on the dependent variable—Hardiness. There was also an increase in the R-squared value from 0.440 to 0.460, which suggests that the inclusion of Culture and its dimensions as independent variables explained more variation and impact on Hardiness than before. Furthermore, the variation in the outcome variable—Hardiness—due to its predictors was more evident when the adjusted R-squared value of 0.433 changed to 0.435 after the addition of Culture. The standard error of estimate was reduced from 0.540 to 0.539.

When Culture was included, the ANOVA results of regression analysis also depicted a significant F value = 18.974, p (.000) < .05. The beta values in the coefficients table suggested that Commitment was the highest contributing (0.515) predictor for explaining Hardiness in these professionals, followed by Challenge (0.190), then PE (0.084), SK (0.081), Control (0.63) and CT (-0.050) in comparison to others. There was no multicollinearity effect among the predictors. Hence, the inclusion of Culture as another significant contributor of Hardiness to the existing model of 3Cs can be considered a good fit model.

From these findings, it can be concluded that culture *does* contribute towards making hardy individuals, thus allowing **Hypothesis 4** to be accepted and fulfilling the fourth objective of my study.

There was no significant difference in the banking and IT professionals who live in Bhubaneswar and Bengaluru cities with respect to the levels of role stress and hardiness they experienced. The cultural differences were also not found between the professionals as far as both the cities were concerned. However, sector-wise, only KY in Indian culture showed significant variation among the IT professionals compared to the banking professionals. Thus, **Hypothesis 5** of this study is partly acceptable.

4.3 Recommendations (Academic and Managerial)

4.3.1 Academic Recommendations

- This is probably one of the first studies relating hardiness to the various aspects of Indian culture. It is a universally acknowledged fact that culture contributes in shaping an individual's personality, but this study helped identify the contribution of culture in making hardy individuals.
- The current research project would be helpful to other scholars and researchers who wish to study the positive effects of hardiness in corporate professionals who undergo stressful situations. Especially for future researchers, the outcomes obtained from this study can be useful in generalising outcomes obtained from studies related to banking and IT professionals.
- The present study is perhaps one of the first endeavours to measure the relationship and interactive effects of corporate professionals' hardiness with GRSs like SRD, IRD, RB, and PIn. The results obtained from this study can be helpful for future researches related to GRS and hardiness.
- Dr Suzanne C. Kobasa developed the concept of hardiness as a personality disposition, but other major researchers in this area of study, including Dr S. R. Maddi, have considered hardiness as a combination of attitudes. Therefore, the concept of hardiness can also be looked at as an important personality disposition and could be included in the course curricula in such subjects as organisational behaviour and human resources management. It can be also added as an important factor in the curriculum of stress management.

4.3.2 Managerial Implications

First, the identification of various work/role stresses is crucial to the healthy physical and mental well-being of professionals working in different corporate sectors and industries. Stress management is very crucial because unmanaged stress can be detrimental to the mental and physical well-being of the professionals as well as the organisations in which they work. Mismanaged stress can also lead to low work motivation, low productivity, absenteeism, and low job satisfaction in working professionals, leading towards the lower overall performance of the organisation.

Second, stress management would be effective only when professionals are trained enough to be hardy in dealing with stressful situations. It goes without saying that stress-hardy people will have an edge over those who do not have this personality trait/attitude. Importantly, those individuals who do not have a hardy personality can actually inculcate it and learn hardy ways of coping. This can be achieved through proper training imparted by experts on a regular basis to professionals. Through proper hardy training, individuals can learn how to control events which occur around them, effectively and react to the challenges faced in a more flexible and confident manner.

S. R. Maddi, one of the pioneering researchers in hardiness has developed this concept and founded his Hardy Institute, Inc. at Newport Beach, California, in the United States, which imparts hardy training dealing with effective hardy coping, hardy skills, and hardy social interactions. This hardy training has proved to be very beneficial to the subjects of various occupations. Thus, such hardiness training would help professionals in effectively coping with stressful situations, leading to more productivity, efficiency, and overall job satisfaction.

4.4 Scope for Future Research

Stress, as we all know, is a major concern in today's competitive, result-oriented corporate world. It is a malady which most individuals also suffer from. Although stress has been a widely taught and researched subject area, there has hardly been enough research on hardiness and even less on its relationship with culture. The study of hardiness calls for a multidisciplinary approach, involving areas of study like human resources management, sociology, psychology, and social psychology, among others. This area of study has scope for further research involving students, teachers, nursing and medical professionals, defence personnel, paramilitary/police organisations, and the like who have to cope with several kinds of stress. Such studies on the implication of hardiness can be helpful in the management of stress in a big way.

Besides, as culture plays an influential role in shaping the personality trait of an individual, there could be future research relating culture as a contributing factor towards making hardy professionals.

4.5 Conclusion

The present study, inspired by Kobasa's theory of hardiness has possibly laid the groundwork for those areas of research in the study of management of stress taking a spatio-temporal object for analysis. It took India and Indian culture and the post-liberalisation era as its primary locus of research and has come up with some new findings which might be helpful not only to future researchers in this area of study but also those working as professionals trying 24/7 to cope with the stress they have to undergo owing to the changed and changing scenarios of the workplaces and job requirements.

As I have already suggested, hardiness can also be taught, and my work might encourage organisations to take up hardiness training in earnest.

No research work can be an end in itself. It is always a continuation of the earlier works done in the field, and if it can stimulate further enquiry by future scholars, my efforts may well be considered aptly rewarded.

References

Almeida, D. M., and Kessler, R. C. (1998). Everyday stressors and gender differences in daily distress. *Journal of Personality and Social Psychology, 75*, 670–680.

Bano, B. (2013). Personality types and its relationship with role stress a study among police personnel. PhD dissertation, Department of Business Administration, Aligarh Muslim University. http://hdl.handle.net/10603/183924

Bartone, P. T. (1984). Stress and health in Chicago transit authority bus drivers. University of Chicago, Chicago, unpublished doctoral dissertation.

Bartone, P. T. (1995). A short hardiness scale. Paper presented at meeting of the American Psychological Society, New York. www.hardiness-resilience.com

Bartone, P. T. (2007). Test-retest reliability of the dispositional resilience scale-15: A brief hardiness scale. *Psychological Reports, 101*, 943–944. www.hardiness-resilience.com

Bartone, P. T. (2013). A new taxonomy for understanding factors leading to suicide in the military. *International Journal of Emergency Mental Health and Human Resilience*, Chevron Publishing, *15*(4), 299–306.

Bartone, P. T., and Priest, R. F. (2001). Sex differences in hardiness and health among West point cadets. Paper Presented at the 13th Annual Convention of the American Psychological Society, Toronto. www.hardiness-resilience.com

Bartone, P. T., Ursano, R. J., Wright, K. M., and Ingraham, L. H. (1989). The impact of a military air disaster on the health of assistance workers: A prospective study. *Journal of Nervous & Mental disease, 177*(6), 317–328.

Beena, C., and Poduval, P. R. (1992). Gender differences in work stress of executives. *Psychological Studies, 37*(2), 109–113.

Claypoole, K. H. J. (1987). The impact of stressful life events on illness rates and immune functioning as moderated by type A behaviour, hardiness, loneliness, nutrition and exercise. Dissertation, University of Wyoming. UMI, Ann Arbor, USA. Retrieved from ProQuest Digital Dissertations.

Cox, T., Kuk, G., and Leiter, M. P. (1993). Burnout, health, work stress, and organizational healthiness. In W. B. Schaufeli, C. Maslach, and T. Marek (Eds.), *Series in applied psychology: Social issues and questions: Professional burnout: Recent developments in theory and research* (pp. 177–193). Philadelphia: Taylor & Francis.

Cronkite, R. C., and Moos, R. H. (1984). The role of predisposing and moderating factors in the stress-illness relationship. *Journal of Health and Social Behaviour, 25*(4), 372–393.

Crowe, L. A. S. (1998). Hardiness, one of several personality constructs thought to affect health. Dissertation, Division of Research and Advanced Studies of the University of Cincinnati. UMI, Ann Arbor, USA. Retrieved from ProQuest Digital Dissertations.

Cushway, D., and Tyler, P. A. (1994). Stress and coping in clinical psychologists. *Stress Medicine, 10*(1), 35–42. https://doi.org/10.1002/smi.2460100107

Decker, P. J., and Borgen, F. H. (1993). Dimensions of work appraisal: Stress, strain, coping, job satisfaction, and negative affectivity. *Journal of Counseling Psychology, 40*(4), 470–478. https://doi.org/10.1037/0022-0167.40.4.470

Duquette, A., Kérouac, S., Sandhu, B. K., Ducharme, F., and Saulnier, P. (1995). Psychosocial determinants of burnout in geriatric nursing. *The International Journal of Nursing Studies, 32*(5), 443–456. https://doi.org/10.1016/0020-7489(95)00006-J

Gerson, M. (1998). The relationship between hardiness, coping skills, and stress in graduate students. Dissertation, Adler School of Professional Psychology. UMI, Ann Arbor, USA. Retrieved from ProQuest Digital Dissertations.

Hannah, T. E., and Morrissey, C. (1987). Correlates of psychological hardiness in Canadian adolescents. *The Journal of Social Psychology, 127*(4), 339–344.

Harilal, A., and Santhosh, V. A. (2017). A comparative study on stress levels among working women and housewives with reference to the state of Kerala. *NMIMS Journal of Economics and Public Policy, 2*(1), 29–35.

Hystad, S. W. (2012). Exploring gender equivalence and bias in a measure of psychological hardiness. *International Journal of Psychological Studies, 4*(4), 69–79.

Kelly, M. B. (1997). The effect of work-related and personal demographic variables on burnout and hardiness in nurse managers. A Thesis proposal presented to the Faculty of the Department of Nursing, Clarkson College. UMI, Ann Arbor, USA. Retrieved from ProQuest Digital Dissertations.

Kenney, J. W. (2000). Women's "inner-balance": A comparison of stressors, personality traits and health problems by age groups. *Journal of Advance Nursing, 31*(3), 639–650.

Kobasa, S. C. (1979a). Stressful life events, personality, and health: Inquiry into hardiness. *Journal of Personality and Social Psychology, 37*(1), 1–11.

Kobasa, S. C. (1981). Barriers to work stress: The hardy personality. In D. Gentry (Ed.), *Behavioral medicine: Work, stress, and health* (pp. 181–204). Martinus Nijhoff Publishers. https://books.google.co.in/books?id=LHehBQAAQBAJ&printsec=frontcover#v=onepage&q&f=false

Kobasa, S. C. (1982a). Commitment and coping in stress resistance among lawyers. *Journal of Personality and Social Psychology, 42*, 707–717.

Kobasa, S. C. (1982b). The hardy personality: Toward a social psychology of stress and health. In G. Sanders and J. Suls (Eds.), *Social psychology of health and illness* (pp. 3–32). Erlbaum.

Kobasa, S. C., Maddi, S. R., and Courington, S. (1981). Personality and constitution as mediators in the stress-illness relationship. *Journal of Health and Social Behaviour, 22*, 368–378.

Kobasa, S. C., Maddi, S. R., and Kahn, S. (1982). Hardiness and health: A prospective study. *Journal of Personality and Social Psychology, 42*, 168–177. http://dx.doi.org/10.1037/0022-3514.42.1.168

Kobasa, S. C., Maddi, S. R., and Puccetti, M. C. (1982). Personality and exercise as buffers in the stress-illness relationship. *Journal of Behavioral Medicine, 5*, 391–404.

Leiter, M. P., Clark, D., and Dump, J. (1994). Distinct models of burnout and commitment among men and women in the military. *Journal of Applied Behavioral Science, 30*(1), 63–82.

Macewen, K. E., and Barling, J. (1988). Interrole conflict, family support and marital adjustment of employed mothers: A short term, longitudinal study. *Journal of Organizational Behaviour, 9*, 241–250.

McDonough, P., and Walters, W. (2001). Gender and health: Reassessing patterns and explanations. *Social Science & Medicine, 52*, 547–559.

Nowack, K. M. (1989). Coping style, cognitive hardiness, and health status. *Journal of Behavioral Medicine, 12*(2), 145–158.

Pareek, U. (2002). *Training instruments in HRD and OD* (2nd ed.), New Delhi: Tata McGraw Hill Publishing Company Ltd.

Parkes, K. R., and Rendall, D. (1988). The hardy personality and its relationship to extraversion and neuroticism. *Journal of Personality and Individual Differences, 9*(4), 785–790.

Payne, J. N. (1990). A study of demographics, role stress, and hardiness in the prediction of burnout among ministers. Dissertation, University of Mississippi. UMI, Ann Arbor, USA. Retrieved from ProQuest Digital Dissertations.

Radisic, J. (2005). Police hardiness and officer's length of service. Dissertation, Chicago School of Professional Psychology. UMI, Ann Arbor, USA. Retrieved from ProQuest Digital Dissertations.

Sandhu, K. S., Sharma, R. K., and Singh, A. (2009). Personality hardiness of Indian coaches in relation to their age and coaching experience. *Journal of Exercise Science and Physiotherapy, 5*(1), 38–41.

Sheard, M. (2009). Hardiness commitment, gender, and age differentiate university academic performance. *British Journal of Educational Psychology, 79*, 189–204.

Snow, D. A. (1995). Personality correlates of adolescent stress coping responses. Dissertation, Michigan State University. UMI, Ann Arbor, USA. Retrieved from ProQuest Digital Dissertations.

Sowa, C. J., May, K. M., and Niles, S. G. (1994). Occupational stress within the counseling profession: Implications for counselor training. *Counselor Education and Supervision, 34*(1), 19–29. https://doi.org/10.1002/j.1556-6978.1994.tb00307.x

van der Pompe, G., and De Heus, P. (1993). Work stress, social support, and strains among male and female managers. *Anxiety, Stress and Coping, 6*(3), 215–229. DOI: 10.1080/10615809308248381

Index

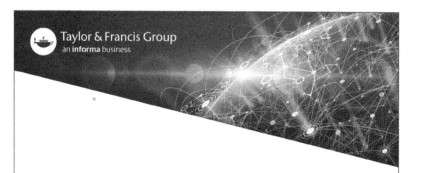